NEW HORIZONS IN JOURNALISM

Howard Rusk Long, *General Editor*

Advisory Board

Irving Dilliard, *Ferris Professor of Journalism*
Princeton University

Jacques Léauté, *Directeur*
Centre International D'Enseignement Supérieur du Jour-
nalisme, Université de Strasbourg

James S. Pope, *Former Executive Editor*
Louisville *Courier-Journal* and *Times*

Donald Tyerman, *Former Editor*
The Economist, London

Hugh Gaine

A COLONIAL PRINTER-EDITOR'S ODYSSEY TO LOYALISM

by Alfred Lawrence Lorenz

Foreword by Howard Rusk Long

SOUTHERN ILLINOIS UNIVERSITY PRESS
Carbondale and Edwardsville

Feffer & Simons, Inc.
London and Amsterdam

Library of Congress Cataloging in Publication Data

Lorenz, Alfred Lawrence, 1937–
  Hugh Gaine: a Colonial printer-editor's odyssey to loyalism.

  (New horizons in journalism)
  Bibliography: p.
  1. Gaine, Hugh, 1726 or 7–1807.   I. Title.
Z232.G2L6   070.5'092'4   72–75335
ISBN 0–8093–0588–7

Printed in the United States of America
Designed by   Gary Gore

To my mother
and the memory of my father

Contents

Foreword

History, long queen of the curriculum in schools of journalism, becomes increasingly unfashionable as younger scholars turn more and more to behavioral studies of contemporary audiences, of the media, and of the writers and policy makers designated as "communicators." Yet until the new communications science produces its fragmentations in sufficient quantity, range, and depth to provide the building blocks of generalization, the historical method remains the indispensable key to an understanding of American journalism, past, present, and future.

For those who look to the past to explain the present and to predict the future, it is fortunate that Professor Lawrence Lorenz, of the Marquette University College of Journalism, has concentrated his scholarly study upon the late Colonial period. This investigation into the life and works of Hugh Gaine delves into sources hitherto unmined by earlier biographers and thus draws newer and finer distinctions in the role and, perhaps, the motives of the man who seemed to find it so easy and so remunerative to serve both sides in the war of the American Revolution. Diligence and a sound intuition enable Lorenz to flesh out the stereotyped "turncoat editor" into a portrait of the living man who, by challenging his destiny, found himself beset by conflicting forces in his social environment. The stereotypes cast aside, Gaine is revealed as a man capable of making compromises reasonable enough for the time and the place, however reprehensible his actions appear in conventional interpretations of the struggle of the American colonies for their freedom.

This book will be read as a valuable addition to the growing bibliography of the Colonial press. But it is much more than that. We see Gaine as a man more concerned with profit than with principle. Thus we learn that the commercial press of today, with so little regard for social responsibility or the rights of the individual who reads, views, or listens, is neither the product of our times alone nor to be found in bigness alone. Moreover, we perceive that few new monopolistic business practices were invented in the period between the eighteenth and the twentieth centuries. In Gaine we see in action the universal businessman, prepared to take his customers as they come, aloof from the consequences of the transaction.

We may smile at the slow pace and petty quarrels of the parochial New York in which Hugh Gaine made his mark; we may compare his clumsy and primitive equipment with the sophisticated hardware available to publishers of today's newspapers, but there is no evidence that people in their relations with each other have changed so very much. If ours is a time of crisis, social conflict, and intolerance—so were the days of Hugh Gaine. Man's inhumanity to man seems neither to have gained nor diminished. If anything, we are the losers because for the people who did not like Hugh Gaine's newspaper, others were available.

HOWARD RUSK LONG

Carbondale, Illinois
May 3, 1972

Preface

֍ In the late summer of 1776, the second year of America's war for independence, the New York printer Hugh Gaine, publisher of the *New-York Gazette; and the Weekly Mercury*, fled the city to escape a threatened British invasion. Setting up a press in Newark, New Jersey, he began printing his newspaper in support of the American revolutionaries. Gaine stayed at Newark only a month and a half, however, and returned to New York on November 1 to enlist the *Mercury* in the British cause.

Gaine's switch in allegiance and his subsequent scurrilous attacks on the American cause through his press made him the target of patriot hatred; historians of American journalism, in their brief mentions, have tended to echo patriot characterizations of him. But Hugh Gaine cannot be so easily dismissed. He was one of the most prosperous of colonial American publishers and his newspaper held a wide readership for more than thirty years. For most of those years, his was the principal newspaper voice of conservatism in the colonies.

This study is an attempt to illuminate Gaine's life and, particularly, to arrive at an understanding of the reasons why he defected to the British. Within the limits imposed by a dearth of personal records, it examines his full eighty-one years, with particular attention given to his thirty-year career as printer-editor of the *Mercury*. In keeping with the main purpose, however, it focuses primarily on Gaine's publishing activities from the passage of the Stamp Act in 1764 to the printer's move into the British camp in 1776.

I am most grateful to a number of persons and institutions who contributed to the making of this volume: to Jim A. Hart, for painstakingly and patiently midwifing the first drafts; to Howard R. Long, Bryce W. Rucker, George W. Adams, Frank L. Klingberg, and Clifford L. Helbert, for their encouragement and valuable suggestions; to the staffs of the Chicago Public Library, the Library of Congress, Morris Library of Southern Illinois University, the Newberry Library, and Trinity Church, New York; and to Marquette University, for providing a summer faculty fellowship which allowed me to complete the work. I would also like to express my gratitude to my wife, Kathleen, for her very special support and encouragement.

ALFRED LAWRENCE LORENZ

Marquette University
May 1, 1972

HUGH GAINE

CHAPTER 1

Apprentice to Publisher

Since early in the previous week the print shop had been filled with activity. The new English common press, just shipped from Britain and freshly uncrated, had been set up. The printer and his workmen had admired its gleaming metal and fresh wood, still unsoiled by printer's ink—but not for long. Fonts of type had been laid in the cases, then taken out again, piece by piece, to spell out in their peculiar upside-down fashion the words which would fill the first page of the newspaper that was scheduled to appear the following Monday. Nearby were stacked piles of paper ready for the press.

Now it was Saturday, August 1, 1752. The press was readied for printing, a proof taken, then all work stopped for the moment while twenty-six-year-old Hugh Gaine, proprietor of the newest printing shop in New York and publisher of what had just become the *New-York Mercury*, studied the sheet.

Gaine, a round-faced, stocky young man in brown homespun—a uniform he would wear through good times and bad—peered at the still damp proof, reading the news items he had ordered printed. Then he gave instructions in his thick Irish brogue: a bit more makeready here; less there; and hurry, the new press would yield only 250 impressions an hour, then the paper had to be hung up to allow the ink to dry before printing on the other side.

As Gaine relaxed the next day after the long preparations, he undoubtedly worried about the reception the *Mercury* would receive
when it was put on sale for the first time Monday morning. But his
happiness must have overshadowed his concern. Only twelve years
from his first day as an apprentice and he was proprietor of his
own shop; only seven years in America and he was publisher of his
own newspaper.

Gaine was born in 1726 in Portglenone, Parish of Ahoghill,
Ireland, northwest of Belfast and on the Bann River a few miles
north of Lough Neagh. He was named for his father, Hugh, but
nothing else is known of the boy's early years; he left no memoirs
or recollections. Judging from his later actions, we can assume that
he was an intelligent youth, perhaps with a temper too easily provoked, and that he probably chafed at the humility and depriva-
tions of poverty. Even in his prosperous days he would wear old
clothes and would fear indebtedness to such an extent that his
neighbors would joke about him.

As he grew into his teens, he and his father doubtless discussed
his future. Was he to farm? to be a shopkeeper? The silversmith's
trade was a profitable one. Whichever way the discussions went,
they came finally to one: the printing trade. The boy had learned
his letters and could write; he enjoyed reading and he was meticu-
lous—the elder Gaine cataloged his son's attributes for the owners
of a Belfast printing house, Samuel Wilson and James Magee,
and they granted that the boy had the qualities they wanted in an
apprentice. And so it was agreed; Hugh would be a printer. Just
eight days before Christmas, 1740, father and son set out for Belfast and the printing shop in Beaver Street at the sign of the Crown
and Bible, and fourteen-year-old Hugh was indentured to Wilson
and Magee for a period of six years.[1]

Gaine's childhood ended as the three men put their signatures
on his apprenticeship paper. Under the terms of the indenture,
Gaine was forbidden any pleasures that might interfere with his
duties at the print shop or cost his masters money. He could not

"play at Cards, Dice, Tables, or any other unlawful Games, Whereby his said Masters may have Loss"; without their permission he could "neither Buy nor Sell," nor could he "haunt any Taverns, Ale Houses, or Play-Houses. . . . But in all Things as an honest and faithful Apprentice he shall behave himself towards his said Masters and all theirs during the said Term." The provisions were strict, especially for a country lad who must have been attracted by the lures of the city, but Gaine honored the rigid rules and in so doing, he would develop habits of diligence and sobriety—habits which would hold him to the path his spurring ambition later marked for him.

Even if Hugh had been less steadfast, it is doubtful that he had time to sample Belfast's pleasures. The indenture also specified that Wilson and Magee, "their said Apprentice, in the same Art which they use, by the best Way and Means that they can, shall Teach and Instruct, or cause to be Taught and Instructed, with due Correction; finding unto their said Apprentice, Meat, Drink, Washing and Lodging befitting such an Apprentice, during the said Term." And he had much to learn.

Gaine mastered the lay of the type case by distributing type from completed jobs and then setting new copy until his fingers grew calloused and no longer ached from the task but fairly flew across the face of the case while plucking out the pieces of metal. He learned the various type sizes: nonpareil, brevier, primer, great primer, and the rest; and he discovered early the perils of spilling, or piing, a stick or form filled with type. He became familiar with the wooden press, knew its operation, and could refer to its various parts with the same ease as the journeymen: the type, when set as it would appear on the printed page, was called a form and rested on a flat stone secured in a recessed bed, or coffin; hinged to the coffin was the tympan, on which the paper rested, and hinged to that, the frisket, which folded over the tympan to hold the paper fast; a crank—called the rounce—was turned to roll the carriage holding the form under the heavy block called the platen; the platen was directly beneath a thick iron screw which, when turned, pressed the

platen down against the tympan and forced paper against type to
make the impression.

The journeymen of the shop taught him how to dampen paper
the night before a job was begun so that it would take an impression more easily; how to mix lampblack and varnish into ink;
how to make and use the pelt- or sheepskin-covered balls of wool
to transfer ink to type; how to place small pieces of makeready
paper beneath the tympan so that the sheet would print evenly.
Gaine grew more proficient in the art of printing as he learned how
to set and justify the type and lock it into forms and how to carry
the locked forms from the imposing stone to the press. As he grew
older and more muscular, he took his turn behind the heavy lever
which turned the huge spindle on the heavy machine to draw the
platen down.

As the years of his apprenticeship wore on, Gaine undoubtedly
began to take on the singular appearance and gait of the eighteenth-
century printer: an overdeveloped right shoulder and an enlarged
right foot, the result of the heavy work of pulling the lever on the
press. By the time he had completed his service, his fellow pressmen would recognize him as a veteran because of the way he
walked, much as sailors knew a fellow seaman by his rolling step.

It was hard work, yet Gaine knew he was fortunate. The printing trade was an exclusive fraternity in Ireland and the number of
apprentices was strictly limited by guild regulations so that every
printer was assured of work. A printer, however, could find a
better place in which to carry on his trade. Ireland was a down-
trodden nation. The first years of Gaine's apprenticeship, 1740 and
1741, were years of famine during which thousands of his
countrymen were threatened with starvation. The country, too,
lay under the fist of a Britain which deliberately crushed all manufacture and commerce so that it could increase its own coffers
through trade. Ireland was no place for a man like Gaine, full of
energy and ambition, and in his few free moments he must have
dreamed of joining the estimated twelve thousand other Irishmen
who were fleeing the country in each of those years. Gaine and his
fellow apprentice, Andrew Steuart, who later had a job printing

shop in Philadelphia and from 1764 to 1766 published the *North Carolina Gazette* in Wilmington, may have ignored the banter of the other workers to talk, from time to time, of emigrating to America. True, emigration was a risk; but it was also an opportunity, and when Wilson and Magee dissolved their partnership in 1744, severing Gaine's apprenticeship a year early, the youth made his farewells at Portglenone and sailed for America.[2]

His family may have worried about him when he first announced his plans to emigrate. No job was promised him before he left, but he had it on good authority that American printers needed good journeymen. And he was so confident of his success that he soon allayed the doubts of his family.

Gaine perhaps had second thoughts on the long journey across the Atlantic. He left no record of his voyage, but other trips took from five to eight weeks. Ships were crowded with men and women who lived out the time precariously from the meager provisions they were allowed to bring aboard. Children cried through the night; stormy weather brought seasickness; the water grew stale and brackish and food spoiled; even some of the healthiest passengers became ill and died and, with only a few hasty prayers, were buried at sea. Conditions became irritable, then intolerable.

But, after weeks at sea, the ship finally sailed around Sandy Hook and into New York harbor. Gaine could see the Union Jack flying over Fort George at the tip of Manhattan Island and, less than a half-mile away, the spire of Trinity Church rising 175 feet into the air above the town. As he debarked and walked atop the smooth, round stones that paved New York's irregularly directed streets, he must have heard groups of men speaking not only English but Dutch.

Indeed, it had been only eighty years since the town was last called Nieuw Amsterdam. Appearing more Dutch than English, the houses, high-peaked and gabled, were built of brick. Many were roofed with tiles. If Gaine had dared to look inside any of these, he would have seen whitewashed walls covered with gilt-framed pictures and contrasting bluish-gray furniture and woodwork. These homes were comfortable in winter, and in summer their occupants escaped the heat by sitting on balconies from which they gazed across the Hudson to the New Jersey shoreline or looked down on their own tree-shaded streets.

On his first day in New York young Gaine could have seen the entire town centered as it was below Wall Street, on the site of the present financial district. By walking a quarter of a mile in any direction he could investigate nearly every one of its two thousand shops and houses. New York was not quite the size of Boston or Philadelphia; at the end of the decade, only four years later, it had only a few more than thirteen thousand citizens. But it competed with Boston and Philadelphia for fine buildings, opulence, and commerce, and already a rivalry and a certain jealousy were growing among the three cities. Business ruled, and markets abounded as in no other place in America.

If he asked about the busy merchants and tradesmen who peopled New York, Gaine probably was told, as one visitor was, that they were honest, punctual, and fair in their dealings. And while they were not as rich, perhaps, as some men in Boston and Philadelphia, every man of industry and integrity who settled there could, in time, live well. Any number of the merchants who sat in comfort high on their balconies could have told the nineteen-year-old printer that they had been as poor as he, "without basket or burden," when they first settled in New York. He decided to stay. As Philip Freneau, the poet of the American Revolution, had him say nearly forty years later in the satirical "Hugh Gaine's Life":

> . . . I . . . came to your city and government seat,
> And found it was true you had something to eat;
> When thus I wrote home—"The country is good,
> "They have plenty of victuals and plenty of wood;
> "The people are kind, and, whatever they think,
> "I shall make it appear, I can swim where they'll sink;
> "Dear me; they're so brisk, and so full of good cheer,
> "By my soul, I suspect they have always new year,
> "And therefore conceive it is good to be here." [3]

CHAPTER 2

The *New-York Mercury*

It was, indeed, good to be in New York; the town was just the place for an ambitious young printer, for it was beginning to hunger after culture to complement its affluence. William Bradford had established the colony's first printing press there in 1693 and, in 1725, its first newspaper, the weekly *New-York Gazette*. Now, only two decades later, New Yorkers were reading three local weeklies. Bradford's original *Gazette* was published by one of his former apprentices, Henry De Foreest; John Peter Zenger was still publishing his embattled *Weekly Journal*, which he had founded in 1733; and James Parker, another former apprentice of Bradford's, was publishing the *Weekly Post-Boy*.[1]

Gaine found a journeyman's position in Parker's shop. There was much work; Parker, who had started his printing business and the *Weekly Post-Boy* three years earlier, was official printer for the province of New York. Gaine stayed with Parker for six years, perfecting his craftsmanship and saving his money and looking to the day when he could be independent. Perhaps he hoped that Parker would offer him a partnership or help set him up in business for himself. He felt he could count on Parker as an ally in such a venture.

Certainly his employer had shown a kindly disposition. Early in

7

1751, when Gaine's brother arrived in New York, Parker housed him for five weeks without charging rent. Later, when the brother could find no work as a shopkeeper, for which he had been trained, Parker offered him a partnership in a shop at Woodbridge, New Jersey. Parker allowed him free use of the house, shop, and Negro slaves at Woodbridge and generously divided the profits; half of the earnings was to go to the brother and the other half was to be divided evenly between Gaine and Parker.

Unfortunately, the brother was not as abstemious as Gaine, and at Woodbridge he drank heavily. As a result, in his short tenure there he lost the partnership £40 and mistreated the Negroes. In February 1752, Parker dissolved the agreement.

The incident may have prejudiced Parker against Gaine and in favor of another journeyman in the shop, William Weyman, a minister's son from Philadelphia, who had also served his apprenticeship under Bradford. Weyman, too, wanted to be his own master, and late in 1751 set out for London, apparently with Parker's blessing, to try to secure financial backing. He had little luck, but the following spring, while he was still in England, Zenger died and Parker bought Zenger's shop. Turning his back on Gaine, Parker offered the printing materials to Weyman on credit.[2]

Gaine was enraged. According to one of Parker's apprentices, Gaine saw the letter in which Parker made the offer and immediately determined to break with Parker and open a shop in competition with him. Always penurious, Gaine from his earnings of $1.12 a week had saved £75. From an unnamed friend he secured additional funds, enough to order a press from London. At the same time, he wrote to Weyman and proposed a partnership; going into business with a two-press shop would give the two men a strong start.

Gaine was impelled into business perhaps sooner than he might have wished. Because houses in New York were leased on May 1, he could not afford to wait for his press or Weyman's reply; if he were to act, it would have to be immediately. He rented a shop, ordered a supply of books and other goods; and in June, anticipating a favorable answer from Weyman, he advertised:

To be sold by Weyman and Gaine, at their House on Hunter's Key, next door but one to Mr. Perry's Watchmaker; Bibles of different Sizes, with and without the Common-Prayers of most sorts, Church and Meeting Psalm Books, History of the New Testament, History of the Five Indian Nations, Account of the Earthquake at Lima, Ovid's Metamorphosis, Virgil, Cornelius Nepos, Mariners Compasses, Scales and Dividers, Writing Paper by the Quire or Sheet; also choice good Bonnet-Papers.[3]

It is not known whether Gaine employed his brother, but Weyman did not join him. Instead, the latter joined Parker in partnership of the *Weekly Post-Boy*. As Gaine later learned, he was well rid of his would-be partner, although at the moment he probably was dismayed. Problems facing even an established printer in colonial America were great, but they undoubtedly seemed overwhelming to the novice publisher.

Although most publishers boasted, as Gaine also did, that their newspapers contained the "Freshest Advices, Foreign and Domestick," news items were seldom fresh by modern standards because of the slowness of transportation. Post riders carried domestic news by horseback across nearly impassable roads. Their arrivals, dependent on the vagaries of the weather, were unpredictable. As already noted, ships spent from five to eight weeks in crossing the Atlantic when conditions were favorable, and longer in winter, making dissemination of foreign news even more erratic.

Until 1768, when John Keating opened his New York Paper Manufactory between the Fly Market and Burling's Slip, New York had no paper mill of its own and Gaine would have to import his paper either from England or Pennsylvania. English paper was expensive and slow in arriving; but neither could the printer place full reliance on the Pennsylvanians, as he admitted later when he apologized to his readers for putting out the newspaper on uncommonly small sheets of paper. It was "out of no Disregard for them," he said, "nor indolence in the Printer; But occasioned by an unforeseen Accident, and the Inclemency of the Weather, which has prevented our receiving the usual supply of large Paper from a neighbouring Province."[4] Pennsylvania paper, too, was expensive, and Gaine would try to reduce the cost by offering rewards to his readers for "good clean dry Linen Rags" which he could then use as barter with his suppliers. Later, he avoided such problems by setting up his own paper mill.

Gaine would find type still more difficult to obtain, for it, too, had to be imported from England. The first type-casting operation in America was not established until 1768, and even then domestic type was not as durable as English. It was not until after the Revolution that printers could fully trust the domestic product.

These problems, however, did not deter Gaine; he was competent and he was determined. His press and types arrived in late summer, and he went furiously about the task of preparing to publish his newspaper.

The first number of the *New-York Mercury* bore the date August 3, 1752; and before long Gaine showed that he had been an apt pupil as an apprentice and a journeyman. At first glance, however, the *Mercury* appeared little different from other newspapers of the period. It measured 8 by 12½ inches, with two columns, but within the year Gaine increased the size to 10½ by 18 inches and a three-column format. The typography, though primitive by today's standards, his readers found clear and readable, and in that respect the *Mercury* contrasted with earlier New York newspapers. Gaine used a type similar to that designed by the eighteenth-century letter founder William Caslon. Following the style of the day, the young publisher used the long *s*, which resembled an *f,* at the beginning and in the middle of words; he began all nouns with capital letters to distinguish them from other parts of speech; and he gave emphasis to some expressions by capitalizing them or setting them in italics, or both. To lend variety to pages of gray columns with their simple label headlines, Gaine adhered to the prevailing style, using ornately flowered capitals to begin some news items, and he inserted occasional woodcuts, particularly in advertisements.

In editorial content, too, the *Mercury* was similar to other newspapers in the colonies. Like other publishers, Hugh Gaine was a printer-editor; his editing function and capabilities were subordinate to his activities as a printer. Unlike the modern editor, he did not have a staff of reporters whom he could assign to cover events. He himself only rarely reported an occurrence or commented in print. Instead, he reprinted news items from other colonial and English newspapers, except for a weekly column of local news under the simple heading "New York." He became expert at culling items which would appeal to the colonials' thirst for news and sense of humor, and he treated his subscribers to a variety of fare.

He gave his readers much news from "home." New Yorkers, as other colonials, still considered themselves Englishmen, subjects of the crown, and cherished their ties with the mother country. Gaine nurtured those ties with what would now seem to be a disproportionate amount of space for news from abroad. He printed transcripts of Parliamentary debates alongside relatively inconsequential reports of minor crimes; major actions of the king were related side by side with petty court gossip.

Not that Gaine entirely neglected domestic affairs. He displayed the official proclamations of the governors and mayors on the front pages of his newspaper. Inside, short items told of fires, natural disasters, robberies, and murders in New York and the other colonies.

Many of the news stories, foreign and domestic, were simply and straightforwardly reported: "We hear from Staten-Island, that on Saturday last, a young Woman there, hang'd herself upon an Apple-Tree." [5] Others were more elaborate and, whether of comic or tragic events, often contained a light, almost flippant twist:

Last Wednesday Se'ennight was a terrible Hurricane of Wind with Thunder, Lightning and Rain, which lasted violent about 4 Hours in the Evening, at the upper Part of the Towns of Dover and Berwick, it blew down about 20 Dwelling Houses and several Barns, no Persons kill'd, but several hurt; it blew the Fence Logs about the Corn Fields into the Woods, several Fields of Indian Corn blown down even to the Roots, many large trees of Oak, Pine, &c. blown down, broke off 2 or 3 Feet from the Surface of the Earth, and in the Middle: The Hurricane run in a Vein about 4 Rod wide in some Places, and ten

Miles long: No more of the neighbouring Towns were affected with it, that we can hear; it is also said, that several Oxen were whirled up in the Air for some Minutes.[6]

Stories of marital strife readily found space in the *Mercury*. One such item from London, reprinted in the November 6, 1752, issue, told of an unnamed seaman on a prize ship who had been brought to court for beating his common-law wife, one Catherine Bromley. However, as she had "from Time to Time stript him of almost all his Prize Money, and then deserted him" to marry one of his fellow pirates, he was discharged and the woman ordered to make restitution. The seaman, however, wanted nothing to do with her; he "swore, with great Vehemence, that sooner than come near her again, he would jump into the Flames of Hell-Fire."

Another London woman, as Gaine related the story in the same issue, was less fortunate than Miss Bromley. She "was carried to the London Hospital, with her Skull broke to Pieces, by a Blow given her by her Husband with a Stick, and tho' immediately trapann'd in several Places, there is not the least Prospect of her Recovery."

In addition to the news stories, interested readers knew that at the bottom of the "New York" column they could find a list of ship arrivals and departures. Below the nameplate, for merchants and traders, the penny-minded publisher always printed commodity prices. And Dutch readers, in Gaine's first years of publishing, now and then could find an item in their native language.

Gaine relied heavily on essays to fill his columns. These generally followed the style set by the *Spectator* and similar English periodicals. Often Gaine reprinted them verbatim from the British prints; in other instances writers in the colonies, slavishly copying the English models, sent him their observations on all manner of subjects: the weather and other topics of scientific interest, religion, the joys of bachelorhood, and similar topics.

Advertising appeared to be almost as important as editorial matter. The *Mercury* quickly became a popular vehicle for New York merchants, and Gaine often devoted two or more of the newspaper's four pages to their advertisements. Some weeks, the advertisements overflowed the *Mercury's* pages and Gaine had to issue one-page supplements printed front and back with notices "inserted at five shillings each." It was not unusual for him to apologize to readers for omitting news items because of the great amount of advertising, although if the volume of news warranted he would occasionally omit advertisements.

Notices for household goods and clothing were most prominent; there were also advertisements for runaway slaves and apprentices; for ship sailings and horse races; for books; and for a myriad of other goods, most of them imported from England. Gaine carried announcements of meetings of the Grand Provincial Lodge of the Freemasons. He had joined that lodge, apparently during his years with Parker, and in 1753 was elected secretary. As such, he had the duty to announce meetings and the freedom to choose the newspaper in which the notices would be printed.[7]

Disgruntled husbands frequently made use of the *Mercury's* advertising space to announce that their wives had left their bed and board and would no longer be able to contract debts in their husbands' names. One John Ellis placed such an ad, but his wife later returned, and Gaine probably chuckled when Ellis entered the printing office a week later and asked him to print a retraction: "Whereas the Advertisement inserted in the *New-York Mercury* of the 15th of October Inst. desiring all Persons not to credit Alice the wife of John Ellis, of this City, Painter, being only the Effect of Passion, the Public are hereby requested to regard it as such." [8]

Crude woodcuts illustrated some of the advertisements: a man, arms outstretched and fleeing two pursuers, denoted a fugitive slave or a runaway indentured servant; a packet boat, full sail, an imminent departure for England or the West Indies; a shoe in a square, the wares of Miligan's Shoe Store.[9]

With so much advertising, the *Mercury* became a profitable venture. But revenue also came in from the ever-lengthening list of books Gaine published each year. Beginning in 1752, he brought out an annual almanac by John Nathan Hutchins. The following year he added an almanac by George Christopher, and in 1754, *The New-York Pocket Almanack*, edited by "Poor Tom, Philo." Sermons and other texts of a religious nature would always be prominent features of Gaine's press, and in 1753 he published *A Scheme for the Revival of Christianity* and Isaac Watt's *Divine Songs for Children.* Among the secular works he printed were Joseph Addison's *Cato,* Robert Blair's *The Grave, A Poem,* and T. Dyche's *A Guide to the English Tongue.* These, standing side by side with the collections of books he imported from England, began to make an impressive inventory.

Visitors to the printing office also found the shelves stocked with such sundries as parchment, quill pens, ink-powder, ink pots, spectacles, penknives, and surgical instruments. Alongside were account books, bills of lading, powers of attorney, bonds, bills of sales, blank "Agreements between Masters and Seamen," and the "Southern & West India Pilot's, Mariner's Calender, and Compass, according to the New Stile." At the printing office, too, Gaine acted as go-between for the sale of slaves and indentured servants.

His shelves overflowing with sale goods and his printing business expanding, Gaine soon began looking for larger quarters. In May 1753, he moved to a shop opposite the Old Slip, around the corner from Hanover Square. As with his later moves, he stayed on the east side of town, near the centers of business activity and communication: the markets, the coffee houses, and the wharves. He could step out his door and visit and gossip with other merchants or with ship captains just arrived from England with the latest news; or he could send an apprentice to a ship to pick up the mail from abroad and know that the boy would be back within minutes.

After only one year of publishing, Gaine had achieved a measure of success; he had faced and learned to overcome, at least partially, the physical problems of publishing. In his second year, he would have to contend with the intricacies of New York politics. Soon after his move to the new shop, he found himself involved in a political-religious controversy over the establishment of a college; and in the midst of that battle he was censured by the New York General Assembly.

CHAPTER 3

Churchmen and Legislators

୫୬ New York had no institutions of higher learning when Gaine emigrated there, but numerous proposals that one be built had long been under consideration. Then in 1746 the Assembly instituted a lottery to raise funds for the establishment of a college—King's College, now Columbia University. When the first of the money was turned over to the board of trustees, seven of whom were Anglicans, Trinity Church, the principal Anglican church in the colony, offered ten acres of land for the campus. But Trinity specified that the president should always be an Anglican and that religious services should be conducted according to the rites of the Church of England. To dissenting churchmen, particularly the Presbyterians, the second largest religious sect in the colony, it appeared that the college would be an Anglican, rather than a public, institution, and serve primarily to insure that Anglican pulpits would be kept filled. Their fears turned to anger in 1753 when the Assembly passed an act to divert funds from an excise tax to the use of the college.[1]

Taking up the cudgel in opposition to any possible Anglican control of the college were three young lawyers, all of them prominent in the revolutionary agitation of ten years later, William Livingston, William Smith, Jr., and John Morin Scott. These three, called "the triumvirate," inaugurated a weekly periodical, *The Independent Reflector;* James Parker agreed to print it for them. When the excise tax proposal came before the legislature, the triumvirate swung into action against it.[2]

Gaine soon discovered that he was a secondary target of the three. He was an Anglican while his fellow Northern Irishmen commonly belonged to the Presbyterian Church of Scotland; and in the triumvirate's view, that made him something of a turncoat. At the same time, they saw the *Mercury* as servile to the Anglican establishment. Putting Gaine to the test, the three asked him to publish an essay and a petition which they said had been signed by a group of Irishman and which argued against a connection between the church and the college. Gaine refused; he said he would not involve his newspaper in politics. Young as he was, he was well aware of the repercussions from government or from special interest groups that could follow.

Despite his eagerness to stay out of the fray, Gaine was dragged in anyway. Smith and Scott sent him a letter condemning his neutrality as a subversion of freedom of the press, which, they contended, "Printers above all men should be solicitous to maintain and encourage." He was not truly neutral, they charged, but "averse to Printing any Thing in favour of the Reflector," and thus, of the Presbyterians. They threatened that unless he published the essay and the petition he would perhaps "find the displeasure of his Friends, of more Importance . . . than the Esteem of his Adversaries."[3]

Gaine decided to risk the displeasure of the *Reflector's* friends; he would not publish the two pieces. The next *Reflector* that came to the print shop attacked Gaine in scathing terms. The triumvirate maintained that "A PRINTER ought not to publish every Thing that is offered him; but what is conducive of general Utility, he should not refuse, be the Author a Christian, Jew, Turk or Infidel. Such Refusal is an immediate Abridgement of the Freedom of the Press." Reading on, Gaine probably reddened with anger; the triumvirate was accusing him of selling out press freedom for personal gain:

Personal Interest indeed has, with many [printers], such irresistable Charms, and the general Good is so feeble a Motive, that the only Liberty they know and wish for, is of publishing every Thing with Impunity for which they are paid. I could name a Printer, so attached to this private Interest, that for the sake of advancing it, set up a Press, deserted his Religion, made himself the Tool of a Party he despised, privately condemned and villified his own Correspondents, published the most infamous Falsehoods against others, slandered half the People of his Country, promised afterwards to desist, broke that Promise, continued the Publications of his Lies, Forgeries and Misrepresentations, and to compleat his Malignity, obstinately refused to print the Answers or Vindications of the Persons he had abused; and yet even this Wretch, had the Impudence to talk of the *Liberty of the Press.* God forbid! that every Printer should deserve so infamous a Character.[4]

Thoroughly aroused by this attack, Gaine broke silence. Sitting down to write, he told his readers he was speaking to them directly only "with the greatest reluctance." He was a printer, not a writer, he said; but "when a man's character and indeed his Means of Subsisting in the World, is in Danger of being taken away by a latent Enemy, (which is worse than stabbing a Man behind his Back) I think it cannot be thought impertinence in him to make his case . . . to the Publick." [5]

Gaine had kept the accusing letter from Smith and Scott private; now he decided to publish it as part of his defense. Referring to it, he said he had not published the two items they had submitted because the signatures on the petition were false. The petition, moreover, was "a Reflection not only upon a particular Set of Men, but on a whole Nation," the Irish and Ireland. The essay, he claimed, was an outright plagiarism, taken from Addison's *Spectator.* To prove it, Gaine placed paragraphs of the tract side by side with nearly identical paragraphs from the *Spectator.*

His defense drew the wrath of *The Occasional Reverberator,* a new periodical established to augment the *Reflector* and also printed by Parker. The first issue, in the form of a letter to Gaine, attacked the printer mercilessly. The authors who "so singularly adorned" the *Mercury,* the writer contended, were fools "neither able nor willing to investigate the Truth"; no less a fool was the author of Gaine's letter. Gaine had put "ill-judged Confidence" in him, for he, in his vindication, "set the Fool's Cap upon [Gaine's] Head, and excited the Laughter of the Town." The *Reverberator* again raised the charge that Gaine was attached only to private interest.

You are not, it seems, sensible of any the least Obligations to promote the interest of society: You have no Motives to render your Press useful to the Public; no Consideration of the Advantages that Mankind may reap from the ART OF PRINTING, and the FREE Exercise of the PRESS; but doubtless expect your fellow Creatures will contribute to your Support, when you have not the least Intention to benefit them by setting up your Business. Strange Principles! absurd Conduct, indeed! in a Person who pretends to a fondness for the *Liberty of the Press."*

The *Reverberator* claimed also that Gaine had deserted his religion, was "a Tool to a Party," obviously the Anglicans, and was, in fact, a liar.[6]

Angry as he must have been, Gaine nevertheless refused to reply in kind. Instead, he printed a letter from a reader to justify his silence. Gaine's statement in his own defense, the correspondent wrote, "was unanimously allow'd to be the Dictates of Justice and Innocence, against the Odium of what was impartially prov'd the greatest Absurdities which Fiction and Prejudice could invent." He cautioned Gaine to pay no attention to "such servile Productions for the future; as the Town is now determin'd to be no more impos'd upon by the ludicrous Essays of a few incorrigible Independents, encouraged by the *Reflector."* If Gaine would only continue his "wonted Diligence, in your own Vocation," he was told, he would soon see his antagonists "set up for laughing Stocks to the Town, and pitiful Marks for every Fool to shoot at." [7]

Fresh from that hassle, Gaine became involved in difficulties of a different sort with the General Assembly. In November 1753, following the suicide of Governor Sir Danvers Osborn, he had extracted from the *Votes of the General Assembly* the instructions given Osborn by the king on the former's taking office and printed them in the *Mercury*. The Assembly ordered the printer before it to explain why he had "presumed" to print parts of its proceedings without permission.[8]

That, however, was only the surface reason for Gaine's summons; the legislators were more concerned because he had brought to light the long and sometimes bitter struggle for primacy between the Assembly and New York's governors. The two had consistently clashed because of the conflicting character of their roles: the governors had to look on New York as part of the whole colonial system, whereas the Assembly had local interests at heart. And while the governors derived their authority from the king, the Assembly had control of the purse and had wielded that power to such an extent that the king, in his instructions to Osborn, had charged it with insubordination. As a result of Assembly actions, the king said, "The Peace and Tranquility of the said Province has been disturbed; Order and Government subverted; the Courts of Justice obstructed, and our Royal Prerogative trampled upon, and invaded in a most unwarrantable and illegal manner." [9] The king's charges, the assemblymen undoubtedly reasoned, might influence voters against them and should be kept secret. With this disclosure made, however, they were determined to punish the Pandora who released the damning instructions.

Gaine could not have been surprised at the summons. While the press in New York in the eighteenth century was generally unrestricted because of the outcome of the Zenger trial of 1734 and 1735 and could publish with only minimal danger of being subdued by the government, the government nevertheless had power to coerce printers. So Gaine made his way up to the Assembly's miniature parliamentary chambers at City Hall at what is now the corner of Nassau and Wall streets. Standing before the twenty-seven imposingly robed and bewigged legislators, he was asked "by what Authority" he had printed the extract. Gaine answered that he "had no Authority for doing it" and added, probably honestly,

that he "knew not that he did amiss in doing so." Then he
apologized for offending the members and "humbly asked their
Pardon." Undoubtedly mindful both of their tradition of press freedom and of Gaine's support of the Anglican majority, the Assembly
only reprimanded the young printer and, after he had paid costs,
released him.[10] Gaine left the chambers humbled; but he was not
entirely intimidated, and he would have his revenge.

But for the moment, sick of sensitive politicians and political
intrigues, Gaine turned his energies to other matters. In May 1754,
he once again moved his shop, this time to a house recently vacated
by a tailor named Anderson, between the Fly and Meal Markets
on the Old Slip, about two blocks north of his former shop. Once
settled he began laying plans for a new publication.

He had read the *Spectator* and similar British periodicals and
doubtless had admired their witty, urbane tone. Now he proposed
to establish a similar magazine in New York. It was to be called
The Plebean and was to be devoted to literary essays rather than
news. The first issue, a single sheet, 12⅛ by 8 inches and edited by
one "Noah Meanwell," came from his press on August 14, 1754.[11]
The Plebean found few subscribers, however. Although New Yorkers could read occasional literary and political essays in the *Mercury* and other newspapers, they had not yet achieved the level of
intellectual sophistication necessary for the success of a solely
literary publication. *The Plebean* died, apparently within its first
year,[12] but any financial setback for Gaine was only temporary.

CHAPTER 4

Printing Away with Amazing Success

⁊⧆⟩ To Gaine's new shop one day in the fall of 1754 came Livingston, Scott, and Smith to appeal to their adversary of a year earlier for help. Gaine might have guessed what they wanted. He knew Parker had stopped printing the *Reverberator* and the *Reflector;* subscribers had threatened to discontinue the *Weekly Post-Boy,* and Parker had worried, too, that he might well lose his post as public printer if the targets of those two magazines, the Anglican-dominated Assembly, insisted on reprisals.[1] Now the three were looking for another outlet for their agitation. They had tried pamphleteering, they told Gaine, but pamphlets they found restrictive; they wanted the larger circulation afforded by a newspaper. Could they have space in the *Mercury?*

Gaine was reluctant. After all, they had stood on opposing political sides in the bitter fight of the previous year. The printer also remembered the sting of the Assembly's reprimand; and he, like Parker, feared their reaction if he were to publish Presbyterian sentiments. But the memory of his humbling for printing the king's letter to Osborn still rankled, and under strong pressure from the three, Gaine at last agreed to print their material—but for a fee. Livingston confided to a friend: "We have at length with great trouble got Mr. Gaine to enter into an agreement with us to allot us the first part of his newspaper for the publication of our thoughts, which we do under the name of Watch Tower." Livingston considered Gaine "a fickle fellow, and easily intimidated." However, he wrote, "we have entered into articles of agreement, in writing, which we hope he will not break through." [2]

While bold enough to make the agreement, Gaine still worried over the impression his turnabout would make, and before beginning the "Watch Tower," he penned an explanation to run in the *Mercury* of November 18, 1754, the issue before the series was to start. He had made the agreement with the triumvirate only out of a concern for freedom of expression, he told his readers. Since the Presbyterian organs had ceased publication, the controversy had become even more intense. Another outlet for discussion was needed, he said; thus, he was making his press available to both factions "provided the Authors will indemnify him, and deposite a *Quantum meruit* [whatever it is worth] for his services." Hedging still more, he pleaded that he was entirely objective and said he wanted his readers "to consider him entirely disinterested in all he prints; and that no man would think him an Enemy to any particular Sect or Religion more than another."

Despite that straight-faced disclaimer, Gaine doubtless was amused by the ironies of the situation. He could almost see the consternation on the faces of the Anglican assemblymen even while he was jingling the Presbyterian coins in his pocket. But he had tacitly admitted, as the triumvirate had contended, that private interest did, indeed, hold irresistible charms and that his self-interest, rather than the ideal of a free press, motivated his announced impartiality.

The first "Watch Tower" essay appeared on the front page of the *Mercury* on November 25, 1754. Although the college had opened in July in the vestry of Trinity Church, the "Watch Tower" writers kept up their attacks against the use of tax money for its support for fifty-one more issues, until November 17, 1755. They had lost the main battle; but they won a partial victory, because the Assembly eventually divided the lottery funds between the college and the city corporation. [3]

For Gaine, the controversy proved especially lucrative. True to his word, he opened his press to the Anglicans as well as the Presbyterians and won contracts for the printing of at least three Anglican pamphlets, all of them stimulated by the long controversy: *A Letter to the Independent Reflector,* by the pseudonymous David Marin Ben Jesse; Francis Squire's *An Answer to Some Late Papers Entitled, The Independent Whig;* and Benjamin Nicoll's *A Brief Vindication of the Trustees Relating to the College.*

But more important than the immediate gains or losses of either faction in the struggle, and of more significance, certainly, than Gaine's printing contracts, the fight over the college anticipated the revolutionary agitation which would begin in earnest ten years later. The position taken by the Livingston-Scott-Smith faction was symptomatic of still deeper grievances against British colonial policy. Gaine's own unsteadiness foreshadowed the position of no position he would try to maintain in the battles ahead.

For the moment, however, Gaine looked ahead to his future in business. In 1755 he raised above his door a sign to advertise his printing shop, as other fine merchants did: a Bible and above it a crown, a variation of the sign he had worked beneath as the apprentice of Magee and Wilson. The name "Bible and Crown" was to identify his business until the end of the Revolution, when he removed the crown; it appeared in the colophon on both the *Mercury* and the books he published and in time it became famous. As Freneau, in "Hugh Gaine's Life," had him boast:

> But what do I say—who e'er came to town,
> And knew not Hugh Gaine at the Bible and Crown.

The Bible and Crown was best known at its location in prestigious Hanover Square, where Gaine moved in May 1757. There, two doors south of the Meal Market, in "the House next Door to Doctor William Brownjohn's" he would do business for the rest of his life, except for a five-month period in 1763 when he took up temporary residence in Rotten Row.[4] Hanover Square was the center of wealth and fashion in eighteenth-century New York, and the new Bible and Crown was as elegant as any of its neighbors—

three stories high, it had two rooms on each floor, a kitchen, a
cellar, and a cellar kitchen for servants. It was too large, in fact, for
the bachelor Gaine to take care of by himself, and he was soon
advertising for "a good house-keeper that can be well-recom-
mended." [5] In all, it was quite an improvement, Gaine could reason,
over the thatched cottage he had known as a boy in Portglenone.

He had never really forgotten those days, however; he still went
about his errands, whether in the shop or in the town, in his old
brown homespun clothes. And among his neighbors he was getting
a reputation for miserliness, although perhaps with too little justification. True, when the New York Assembly in 1756 passed a
newspaper tax of a half-penny on each week's issue of the *Mercury*,
Gaine made his readers pay for the levy; and two years later he
had them absorb fees ranging from nine cents to one shilling, six-
pence to be paid post riders for delivering the newspaper out of
town. But in doing so, he was acting no differently from other publishers, and when the 1756 tax expired in 1759, Gaine reduced the
cost of the *Mercury* accordingly.[6] Perhaps he did worry too much
and too publicly that those same subscribers would not pay
promptly; quite frequently he reminded them in print to "discharge their accounts as soon as convenient, by which he will be
enabled to pay his own lawful debts, and serve his Friends as
formerly." [7] But, in any event, he was achieving a reputation as
something of an eccentric in money matters.

He was, however, a skillful editor; and as time went on, he provided his readers with an ever-improving newspaper, as they could
notice in his coverage of the French and Indian Wars. The wars
had been renewed in 1754, only six years after the Treaty of Aix-
la-Chapelle had ended King George's War; they had started this
time on North American soil, and readers hungered for news from
the battlefields. At the beginning of hostilities, in May 1754, Gaine
had reproduced from the *Pennsylvania Gazette* Benjamin Franklin's famous serpent device which warned the colonists to "Join or
Die." As hostilities continued, he carried as much news about the
war as his correspondents, army officers in the field, could write and

his columns could bear. He was also enterprising enough that when news came of Colonel George Washington's surrender of Fort Necessity to the French, he printed an extraordinary edition to get the news on the street before the next regular issue of the *Mercury*.

Gaine himself, as a member of the militia, took part in at least one foray against the enemy. In August 1757, three months after the printer's move to Hanover Square, the Marquis de Montcalm, the French commander in North America, attacked and overwhelmed Fort Oswego on Lake Ontario, and Fort William Henry at the southern tip of Lake George. The war was drawing perilously close to Manhattan, and authorities and civilians alike grew alarmed. When a militia was formed Gaine enlisted, and on August 14 he and what he described as "many more Volunteers, in the service of their Country," marched to Albany to reinforce the regulars in case of a French attack. But he did not see action and returned within the week.[8]

Perhaps he had been in no position to observe details enough to make an interesting story, perhaps he was too busy to write one when he returned, but he passed up the opportunity to be a war correspondent and did not himself report the force's march. He only explained to his readers the reason for the one-week gap in publication that had resulted, and he printed with it the account of an unnamed officer whose letter came by "Express" from Albany.

A year later, the *Mercury* reported the fall of Louisburg to the British, and in a novel experiment, Gaine accompanied the account with a woodcut map of the battle area. He explained to his readers

We hope the following Draught of the City and Harbour of Louisbourg, will be acceptable to our Readers, as it may serve to give them an Idea of the Situation and Strength of the Place, and render the News from thence more intelligible.[9]

The following year, 1759, Gaine reported the greatest event of the war. In the *Mercury* of September 17, 1759, he printed the good news that the French had been defeated on the Plains of Abraham. He did not illustrate the story; but indicative of the newspaper's importance as an advertising medium, he found it necessary to include with the latter report an apology: "We hope those of our Customers whose Advertisements are omitted this Week, will not take it amiss, it being occasioned by the agreeable Advices received from the Fleet and Army at Quebec."

The war also brought Gaine a number of printing contracts, including the Duke of Cumberland's *Standing Orders; A New Exercise, to be Observed by his Majesty's Troops on the Establishment of Great Britain, and Ireland;* the Militia Act of 1758; and the Reverend Abraham Keteltas's sermon, "The Religious Soldier: or, the Military Character of King David." And to the shelves of the Bible and Crown he added "brass-mounted Broad swords . . . so that the purchaser, in case of a French war, will have the advantage of his enemies, as he can encounter them with their own weapons." [10]

In the meantime, Gaine had decided it was time to take a wife. Now thirty-three, he was courting one Sarah Robbins, and she consented to marry him. Then his landlord, Bartholemew Skaats, died. In disposition of the estate, the house in Hanover Square was to be sold, and Gaine was threatened with eviction. He hurriedly raised £975 and bought the house from Skaats's executors. On October 24, 1759, he and Sarah were married at Trinity Church, and he took her home to the living quarters above the printing office. Two years later Sarah gave birth to a daughter, Elizabeth, and in 1762 to a son, John R.

The printer was well able to provide for his new family. He boasted honestly that the *Mercury*, "at Twelve Shillings per Annum," was carried throughout the colonies and even abroad; it went "to every Town and Country Village in the Provinces of New-Jersey, Connecticut, Rhode-Island, and New-York; to all the Capital places on the Continent of America, from Georgia to Halifax; to every Island in the West Indies, and to all the Sea Port

Towns and Cities in England, Scotland, Ireland and Holland."[11]
Clearly he was the leading publisher in New York. He was also
New York's leading bookseller, with competition only from
Garrat Noel. Then, in September 1760, James Rivington appeared on the scene. A penchant for betting on slow horses had lost
Rivington his interest in his prosperous London publishing firm,
and after declaring bankruptcy, he emigrated to America. He arrived early in 1760 and went first to Philadelphia, where he opened
a bookstore in Market Street. Seeking to expand his business, he
took the stage north to New York. Arriving there in the early
autumn of that same year, he began to advertise himself as a "Bookseller, From London."[12]

Gaine and Rivington could not have been expected to be com-
patible or even to like each other. An economic and social gulf
separated their backgrounds: an Englishman of the upper middle
class, Rivington, with his brother, had inherited his father's bookselling business before starting the bankruptcy-doomed firm of his
own. His flamboyance contrasted as sharply with Gaine's sober
habits as his powdered wigs, lace cuffs, and polished manners differed from the Irishman's patched brown homespun and rough,
peasant ways. Within months after Rivington's arrival, the two
were feuding publicly in their advertisements.

Rivington took space in the *Mercury* of April 27, 1761, to advertise that his was "the only London Book Store" in New York.
Although he had never made the claim before, Gaine now stated in
his advertising that his was "the ONLY OLD LONDON BOOK-STORE"
in the town. The two thus identified themselves for the next two
months until, on June 29, Gaine dropped the "only" from his title.
Rivington could have let it go at that; but on July 6, in one last
sally, he loftily proclaimed himself "The ONLY LONDON BOOK-
SELLER, in AMERICA." Gaine shortly after dropped all pretensions
to being a "London" bookseller and Rivington followed suit.[13] The
two men henceforth would find their careers intertwined and Gaine
would find reason again to resent the newcomer.

In one endeavor, Gaine had no competition; he was the city's first and, for a time, only broker of theater tickets. On November 18, 1761, the Chapel Street Theatre opened its doors with the production of the play *The Fair Penitent,* by Nicholas Rowe. Gaine advertised the play in the *Mercury* of November 16, noting that "NO MONEY will be taken at the *Door,* nor any Person *admitted* without TICKETS, which are to be sold by H. GAINE, Printer, at the Bible and Crown, in Hanover-Square." Box seats were eight shillings, places in the pit, five shillings, and in the gallery, three shillings. From that time forward, Gaine would take an active interest in the New York theater.

As his first ten years as a publisher ended, Gaine was in solid circumstances. The *Mercury,* his book trade, and the sale of stationery, pens, and other goods all provided him with a comfortable living. At the same time, he was achieving a measure of personal prestige in the community; in the poll list of 1761, Gaine was called on to serve as an elector. It was not without good reason that Philip Freneau would have him say of those first years:

> . . . I put up a press,
> And printed away with Amazing success;
> Neglected my person, and looked like a fright,
> Was bothered all day, and was busy all night,
> Saw money come in, and the papers went out,
> While Parker and Weyman were driving about,
> And cursing and swearing, and chewing their cuds,
> And wishing Hugh Gaine and his press in the suds.

His outlook for the future seemed even brighter. The Seven Years' War was drawing to an end, and New York and the other colonies appeared ready to enter a new era of prosperity, which the colonists would share. Britain's treasury, however, had been severely weakened by the war, and her leaders were determined that the colonials should bear a substantial portion of the burden of retaining a military establishment in America. As a result, it would not be long before Gaine would find himself fighting for what he saw as his economic survival.

CHAPTER 5

Prelude to a Revolution

꒛꒚ To mark the start of his second decade of publishing, Gaine, on November 15, 1762, ornamented the nameplate of the *Mercury* with the royal coat of arms. Otherwise, the newspaper was little different from the *Mercury* of ten years earlier. It was the same size and still retained its three-column format; the British newspapers remained the source for most of the news items, and essays patterned after those in *Spectator* consistently filled its pages.

Gaine's competition for readership had changed somewhat. Henry De Foreest, who had inherited William Bradford's *Gazette,* had changed the name of that newspaper to the *Evening Post* in 1745, and about the time that Gaine began publishing, he discontinued it entirely. James Parker temporarily retired in 1762. He retained financial control of the *Weekly Post-Boy,* but left its operation in the hands of John Holt.[1] Holt had come north in 1754 from his native Williamsburg, Virginia. He had been a merchant and mayor of the town, but financial reverses forced him to seek another position. Probably through the influence of relatives— he was a brother-in-law of William Hunter, public printer of Virginia—he obtained appointment as deputy postmaster under Parker, who had just been named postmaster at New Haven, Con-

necticut. When Parker established the *Connecticut Gazette* there in
that same year, he took on Holt as editor and junior partner. Six
years later, in 1760, Holt moved to New York and became a
junior partner in James Parker and Co. Now, in 1762, he had
leased Parker's printing business and his newspaper to become a
business rival to Gaine; later, they would become political enemies.[2]

William Weyman, who, it will be recalled, chose to go into
partnership with Parker rather than with Gaine in 1752, was the
third major publisher in the city. He had broken with Parker in
1759 and had begun publication of the *New-York Gazette*.[3] Weyman, however, was an indifferent craftsman and a careless businessman, and the *Gazette*, as we shall see, would fail before the end of
the 1760s.

Two other printers attempted to enter the field in 1762 and 1763.
Samuel Farley began publication of the *American Chronicle* in
New York on March 20, 1762, but a fire which nearly destroyed
his printshop brought the newspaper to a premature end on July
22 of the same year. Another printer, Benjamin Mecom, came down
from Boston, where he had had a printing business since 1757,
and in 1763 established the *New-York Pacquet*. Mecom, a nephew
of Benjamin Franklin, had received financial backing from his
uncle.[4] But he ceased publication within the year, moved to New
Haven, secured the postmastership once held by Parker, and revived the *Connecticut Gazette*.

Despite the newspaper failures, readership was increasing. Americans devoured news, as was testified to by a spoof Gaine published
in the *Mercury* on February 28, 1763. Entitled "Mrs. Buckskin's
complaint of her husband's politics," it had come to the Bible and
Crown in the form of a letter to the printer:

I am an unhappy poor woman, the wife of a journeyman Breeches
maker, who is stupified with snuff, and quite crazy with politics.—I
have three children half naked, and if three half pence would purchase
the reversion of an empire, I am not able to advance a single sixth of
it.—My husband, you must know, Mr. Printer, is a great reader of
news papers, and Monitors and Auditors, and other periodical publications from which he has imbibed a passionate fondness for an

alehouse, and an utter aversion for his work.—In the morning he
steps out for his pint of purl to the Red Lion, without ever considering whether my children and I have a bit of breakfast, and after
chattering the whole morning about the taking of the Havannah, or
the recovery of Newfoundland, comes home to sleep without the least
consideration about providing us a dinner.—My landlord's son who is
apprentice to an apothecary, has obliged me with writing this letter,
and he says, it will be the best way to give you a clear idea of my
husband's behaviour, introducing a specimen of our conversation.—
Suppose then, Mr. Printer, that you see him just come home from his
politics and purl, to take an hours sleep, by way of discharging the
fumes of the liquor, and the drowsiness of his arguments:—he squats
down upon the bedside, and while he takes off his shoes, "Bett, says he,
I am afraid they won't keep the Havannah.

Lord! Buskin, says I, what is it to us whether they keep it or not.
—Haw, (replies he, interrupting me) have you no regard for the
interest of your country? I wish, says I, you had some regard for the
welfare of your family, twould become you better by half.—There's
Jacky has not a stitch of shoes to his feet.—Tommy has broke out with
the itch, and I have got my death of cold for the want of my under
petticoat.—The people at the chandler's shop won't give me credit for
another roll, and the landlady has already given us three different
warnings: there's—

Zounds, Bett, interrupts he what signifies all this to the good of our
country: an English man should die for the good of his country, aye,
that he should, dame, Old England against the world.

Ay, but you sorry fool, says I, is destroying yourself, bringing your
family on the parish, any proof of your regard for your country?
—You are in a pretty fair way of starving for country, I can tell you,
for there is not a single morsel in the house.

To this information, totally insensible, he pays no manner of attention—but goes on—that monitor is certainly a clever fellow, and
so is that North Briton; and the like.

Here, Mr. Printer, not able to bear with him any longer, I generally
fly out in a passion, and make use of some expressions that might
possibly bring no credit on your paper.—If you print this letter, 'twill
expose him at the Red Lion, and perhaps, shame may have a better
effect upon him than all the reasonings of your most humble

                                                ELIZ. BUCKSKIN

The demand for other output of Gaine's press kept pace. In 1762, the New York Assembly contracted with him to have him print its votes and proceedings, which he would publish in two volumes, the first in 1764 and the second in 1766. He also published in 1762 an edition of *Aesop's Fables,* Francis Hopkinson's *Science, a Poem,* a collection of hymns by Isaac Watts, and, of course, a variety of almanacs: *Hutchin's Improved,* Richard Moore's *New-York Pocket Almanack,* and the *New-York Royal Sheet Almanack.*

To the shelves of the printing office, already crammed with pens, paper, and other writing supplies, Gaine added patent medicines. Beginning in 1762 he stocked, among others, "Turlington's Original Balsam of Life . . . an excellent medicine in Decays of Nature, inward Weaknesses and Broken Constitutions"; "Dr. Ryan's Incomparable Worm-Destroying Sugar Plumbs . . . one of the best purges in the whole World for gross bodied Children that are apt to breed Worms, and have large Bellies"; "Dr. Radcliff's Only True Specific Tincture for the TOOTH-ACH, and all disorders in the Teeth and Gums"; "Princely Beautifying Lotion"; and "The Balsam of Honey, and the Essence of the Balm of Gilead, Or, Nature's Grand Restorative." [5]

On the first of May 1763 Gaine temporarily moved the Bible and Crown to the corner opposite the Merchant's Coffee-House in Rotten Row. Why he moved is not known; but it is possible that because of the expansion of his business he was having the house in Hanover Square renovated or enlarged; he may even, at this time, have added another press to the shop. But whatever the reason, he returned to Hanover Square five months later and in the October 3 issue of the *Mercury* advertised that, as of that day, he was back at "the House he formerly occupied in *Hanover-Square;* where, as usual, all Persons may be supplied with *Books* and *Stationary Ware,* on the most reasonable Terms."

Gaine did not want for customers for his varied stock. New York in the *Mercury*'s anniversary year was growing ever more impressive and important. As Gaine hustled about its streets conferring with other businessmen and listening for bits of news with

which to fill his "New York" column, he may have reflected, as
the visitor Andrew Burnaby did, that it was "tolerably well built."
Nearly a thousand new buildings had been erected during Gaine's
twenty years in the city and now almost three thousand homes and
shops filled its narrow, clean streets. Gaine knew its landmarks as
well as he knew the lay of the type case: the charity school, the
workhouse, the prison, the city hall, and the barracks which housed
a regiment of soldiers. Soon there would be another landmark; one
wing of King's College was complete and in 1760 seven young
men had taken their degrees there. Gaine already may have been
making plans to enroll young John in the school, but he may have
wished that a better location could have been found for it. To enter
their classrooms, students had to pass through one of the streets
where the most noted prostitutes of the city lived.

The spires of a dozen churches punctuated the skyline. The two
main churches of the city were Trinity, where Gaine and his family
worshiped, and St. George's Chapel, both Anglican. Other churches
reflected the city's relative toleration for dissenting sects: two
belonged to the Low Dutch Calvinists, one to the High Dutch
Calvinists, and one to the French Calvinists. German Lutherans,
Presbyterians, Quakers, Anabaptists, and Moravians also were
represented; and although the Protestants would tolerate no Catholics, the Jewish population had a synagogue.

More than half of the population was still Dutch, even in 1763,
a century after the English had taken control of the colony; but
the Dutch had so intermingled with the English and other national
strains that the Reverend Burnaby was hard put to give New
Yorkers "any precise or determinate character." He did note, however, that they were "habitually frugal, industrious, and parsimo-
nious" [6]—a description which well fit Gaine. Trade was both vocation and avocation with the predominant merchant class, who
carried on an ever-expanding business from their "safe and convenient harbor." [7] Their city had surpassed Boston in size, if not
in wealth, though Philadelphia was still the first city on the continent.

But New Yorkers, like the other colonists, were growing beyond mere sectional rivalries. Some among them had an idea—"strange as it is visionary," Burnaby said—which would determine, in part, America's response to the crises which loomed just ahead. It was the idea "that empire is travelling westward; and everyone is looking forward with eager and impatient expectation to that destined moment, when America is to give law to the rest of the world." [8] First, however, England was to try to give law to them.

When George Grenville became King George III's prime minister in 1763, he immediately set about the task of making Americans share in the support of British civil and military establishments in the colonies. His Sugar Act, a revision of the Molasses Act of 1733, was designed to do just that. Although the act halved the duty on molasses, it raised sugar duties generally, forbade importation of foreign rum, levied new, high duties on some luxury items imported directly into the colonies, and placed a number of domestic items on the "enumerated" list of colonial products which could be exported only to England.

Immediately the colonials began to oppose the new act on two fronts. On the one hand, they petitioned Parliament for repeal; on the other, they instituted a boycott of the dutied goods and began a drive to replace those goods with domestic products. Gaine took part in both efforts.[9] Almost as soon as the packet boat bringing the act docked, Gaine was setting the provisions in type to distribute as a pamphlet. As petitions against the act flowed from colonial pens, he printed them in the *Mercury*. In the newspaper, too, he gave major support to the campaign to develop home manufactures.

When hints of the strictures of the act had first reached America, one of Gaine's correspondents had taken hope in the country's ability to sustain itself. "Indulgent Nature," the unnamed writer observed in the *Mercury* of January 23, 1764, "has abundantly provided this Country with the Necessaries of Life"; if required, the colonists could draw on those to "set on Foot home Manufactures, which perhaps may not serve the Ends of Pomp and Shew so well as the dear bought Produce of the different Quarters of the World, received by us under so many ruinous Disadvantages, yet many sufficiently answer the Service of Decency and Warmth." Now the colonists began to make his words a reality. New Yorkers established "The Society for the Promotion of Arts, Agriculture and Oeconomy," which awarded prizes for the production of such goods as flax, hemp, potash, linen yarn, and cloth, and for the growing of apple trees, mules, barley, and thorn hedge.[10]

Although there is no record that Gaine was a member of the society, he sympathized with its aims and backed it in print. Certainly with his frugal habits he must have approved privately, as well as publicly, of the society's request that the colonists eschew extravagance: to conserve cloth, none of its members was to mourn for more than six months or, as was the custom, to give scarves— except to the clergy—or serve hot wine at funerals; none was to hire or buy the services of any worker who could not produce a recommendation from the person he had last served in the colony.[11] Gaine further supported the society by praising those who conserved. One such item, printed in the issue of December 24, 1764, read: "A Gentleman in this City whose only Son was interred last Night, appeared at the Funeral without any other mourning than a Hat-band, and the Bearers without Scarfs." Another story, which Gaine related on November 12, 1764, told of a man from New Jersey who had brought to New York "a piece of Brown Linen . . . superior in Strength, and of as even a Thread as any imported." Occasionally, to help ease the burdens of his readers' sacrifices, Gaine entertained them. In the December 24, 1764 issue of the *Mercury* he editorialized that he would like "the agreeable pleasure of seeing some of our patriotic Ladies dress'd in our own Manufacture," and printed alongside his own comment a chiding note from one "Sophia Thrifty":

While you Men will be silly enough to admire a brilliant Figure beyond a prudent Girl, and prefer external Ornament to intrinsic Merit, we Women will be politic enough to spread the most alluring Snare: But remove the Cause (as my Grandfather used to say) and the Effect will cease.—In a Word, down with your Beaux, and the Belles will instantly decrease.

In a subtle protest of his own, Gaine removed the royal arms from the nameplate of the *Mercury* on November 7, 1763, and replaced them with a cut of the mythological god Mercury.

Although resistance to the act continued unabated, Parliament ignored it. The British ministers not only were determined to extract revenue from America but they also considered the colonials well able to pay it. From one of Gaine's correspondents in London came word that news of colonial "Gaiety and Luxury, has reached your mother Country; and they infer from thence your Opulency, which is further confirmed by the extravagant Expences of your Youth sent here for Education." It was also imagined in government circles "that the inhabitants [of America] have received the account of the new duties on several of their productions, with more compliance than was at first imagined, being assured the said income will be appropriated for the good use of the colonies." [12] To Gaine, the statement was "A vile Slander!" [13] But the ministry, heartened by what they believed to be acceptance of the Sugar Act, made plans for other duties. From London came a dire prediction:

You'll soon have a Parcel of Marmadonian Ravens, who will feed upon and rip up your very Vitals, such as Officers of Stamp Duties, Appraisers of Lands, Houses, Furniture, &c. The ministry are determined to make you pay for the Peace which you like so well; the People here find so much fault with it, that they are fearful to load them with any more Taxes.[14]

The first of these "Marmadonian Ravens" to come would be officers to enforce a new and even more onerous tax, the stamp tax. If king and Parliament assumed that the Americans would accept the new levy quietly, as dutiful subjects, they were mistaken. The newspapers of America would lead an outburst of resistance for which the British leaders could not have been prepared. Gaine, his own livelihood challenged by the tax, would stand in the front lines in the propaganda battle ahead.

CHAPTER 6

No Stamped Paper to be Had

🐟 Hugh Gaine must have been a happy man during most of 1764, despite his agitation over the more stringent British colonial policy. His children were growing: Elizabeth was three and John, two. And he and Sarah were expecting another child. On September 14, she gave birth to a girl, whom they named Anne. But the father's joy was to be short-lived; Sarah died—whether in child-birth or soon after is not known—and for five years Gaine had the sorrowful responsibility of raising his three small children by himself.

While Gaine adjusted to the lonely life of a widower in New York's bitterly cold winter of 1764–65, the government in London was devising the Stamp Act, which Parliament passed in March 1765, and which was to go into effect the following November 1. The first direct, internal tax Parliament had laid on the colonies, the stamp tax was, in fact, the first levy of any kind, other than customs duties, which the colonists had to pay to England. Un-fortunately for its perpetrators, as they would soon learn, the act taxed the most influential groups in the colonies: businessmen and merchants, lawyers, clergymen, and printers. The latter, above all, were hard hit; for every newspaper, broadside, pamphlet, almanac, and book—every item to issue from their presses—would have to bear a tax stamp. As a sop to the colonials, Americans were to be appointed agents for distributing the stamps to those who applied for them and for collecting the duties; but that provision did little to soften colonial anger.[1]

The response of the Americans was immediate, articulate, and violent. In the Parliamentary debate over the stamp measure, the Irishman Isaac Barre had referred to the Americans as "Sons of Liberty."[2] Now, while businessmen and merchants organized formal "Sons of Liberty" bands which would physically prevent the sale and use of the stamps, lawyers and clergymen took up their pens to argue against the wisdom and constitutionality of the act; Gaine and other printers set the resulting polemics in type and distributed them in newspapers, broadsides, and pamphlets. Like his fellow publishers, Gaine received these essays in nearly every mail; when he ran short of copy, he had only to pick up any of the exchange newspapers which came to the Bible and Crown from neighboring colonies to find other expressions against the act. Apart from the newspaper, he published the Stamp Act as a pamphlet and printed "Oppression: A Poem," which attacked the act in verse.

Even before passage of the act, he had printed on January 28, 1765, a long section of one essay in the series "The Rights of the Colonies Examined," by Stephen Hopkins, one-time governor of Rhode Island and a partner in the publication of the *Providence Gazette* and *Country Journal.* Although Hopkins protested primarily against the Sugar Act, he also attacked the then-imminent Stamp Act in scathing tones and voiced the prime argument against it: the Stamp Act clearly would be unconstitutional, Hopkins wrote, because direct taxation without the consent of the people was tyranny.

The printer also published articles in support of the British counterargument, that Americans had *de facto* representation in Parliament because members did not merely represent their own constituencies, but the whole empire. A dozen years later Gaine seriously advocated the British position, but in 1765 he set it forth because, as he said, "to be well acquainted with those Arguments, in Support of Measures which so nearly concern us, is undoubtedly desired by every judicious Reader." [3]

Gaine himself wrote no essays refuting the British thesis, but he supplemented the efforts of his contributors by printing news stories which indicated that Parliament had all but ignored American interests during its consideration of the Stamp Act. On April 15, 1765, he printed from the Votes of the House of Commons of two months earlier the resolution on the act agreed to by the House. Along with the extract, he printed two accounts of the deliberations from observers in London who gave the impression that none of the members had spoken on America's behalf during debate on the resolves. On October 28, 1765, only days before the act was to take effect, he recounted in the *Mercury* the gist of a conversation with a ship's captain, a Captain Davis. The British, Davis told Gaine, were so engrossed in their own internal affairs that they had ignored the colonists' "most just and heavy Complaints of Oppression." This, Gaine told his readers, "may serve as an example to show the Absurdity of the Pretence of our being represented by those who can feel no Part of the Burdens and Distresses they would impose on us."

Although the essayists who appeared in the *Mercury* centered their attacks on the concept of "taxation without representation," they voiced other objections as well. "Marlu Aurelius," for example, on November 18, added that although the revenue gathered by the act was to be used to recompense Britain in part for its aid to North America in the war, the colonials had made up the greater part of the fighting forces and had been clothed, even armed, and paid, by the colonial assemblies. Moreover, the war had been fought not for the benefit of the colonies, but of English trade.

John Morin Scott, one of the Presbyterian triumvirate during the struggle over the college, avowed his love and respect for English rule, as most other writers did. But, writing as "Freeman," he stated that the Stamp Act "was calculated to bereave us of the most

valuable Rights we derive from Nature, and the English Constitution," the rights of people to tax themselves. Pride alone dictated
noncompliance with the act, he wrote, for what could the king "or
any Man of Sense, Spirit, and Honesty, think of us, if after we are
so fully convinced of the illegality and devilish Nature of the
Stamp-Act, we yet submit to it?" No revolutionary, Scott nevertheless urged the colonials to oppose the act "with all our might,
even tho' Death should be the Consequence." [4]

"Cato," writing from New Haven, on August 26, exhorted:
"Some, I hope there are . . . that feel the Patriotic Flame glowing
in their Bosoms, and would esteem it glorious to die for their
Country!" Previously, the colonials had thought of England as
their country. Now they began to awaken to the fact of their own
separate existence, and England was emerging as a threat, if not an
enemy, to their aspirations. Gaine furthered such sentiments. For
example, on October 21 he printed an essay by an unnamed writer
who compared the mother country to the hated French and closed
with a verse:

> Ah! my dear country, curst in peace,
> Why did you wish the war to cease;
> The war in which you strew'd the plain,
> With thousands of your heroes slain.
> When Britain to your bleeding shore
> Impetuous pour'd her squadron's [*sic*] o'er;
> And snatch you from the Gallic Brood
> To drink herself your vital blood!

In the same issue, Gaine printed a sermon which had been de-
livered in 1755, during the war against the French, by a Dr. Smith
of Philadelphia. In his homily, the clergyman had reminded British
Americans of their great heritage of freedom and asked: "Shall we
tamely suffer the pestilential breath of tyrants to approach this
garden of our fathers, and blast the fruit of their labours?"

These writings, with their thinly veiled references to revolution,
produced the desired results, especially among the Buckskins. Gaine
was soon detailing, in the most favorable terms, what historian

Arthur Schlesinger, Sr., called the "propaganda of the fist," [5] the physical violence exercised by the recently organized Sons of Liberty. In later years, Gaine was repulsed by the activities of the Sons of Liberty; but not yet. Now he publicized their meetings and gave space to their official notices; more important, he missed few opportunities to report the harm they inflicted on those who appeared ready to observe the provisions of the act. With obvious relish, he reprinted from a Boston newspaper an account of the forced departure from that city of "the most reputable STAMP MAN, attended by his Brother Functioner of this Province, amidst the Exclamations of the People." In Boston, too, Gaine reported, "was exhibited on the Great Tree in the High street in the Town, the Effigies of a DISTRIBUTOR OF THE STAMPS, pendant." [6]

When James McEvers quit his post as collector of the stamp duties in New York, Gaine congratulated "our Countrymen upon the late Resignations of the Stamp Officers—and especially the Friends and well-wishers of the Gentleman appointed to that Office in this City. The Number is greatly increased by his Resignation." Mindful of New York's rivalry with Boston, he condescendingly pointed out that McEvers's resignation was entirely voluntary "and not the Effect of any Menace of Disturbance." But, to forestall any feeling in Boston that New York was less than militant, he added that "it would be no more safe than honourable for any other Person here to attempt to exercise that Office." [7]

Almost gleefully, Gaine recounted on January 27, 1766, the story of Peter Van Schaak of Albany, who had refused to swear to a group of the Sons of Liberty that he would never apply for the hated stamps. A group broke into Van Schaak's home, searched it, and committed "some Outrages on the Furniture, Windows and Balcony; which latter, tho' a very elegant Piece of Work, was entirely demolished." The hapless Van Schaak, Gaine noted, subsequently sent the Sons of Liberty an affidavit that he would not buy stamps.

Such events took place throughout the colonies with a unity which had not existed since the days of the Seven Years' War. A writer whose letter appeared in the *Weekly Post-Boy* as well as in the *Mercury* expressed the emerging sentiment: the colony which submitted to the Stamp Act "will not only appear to the others, in the most groveling and despicable light, but also with great propriety, will be esteemed amongst its most formidable enemies." [8]

As November 1 neared, Gaine and his fellow publishers must have been surprised to find that they were not only reporting events, but influencing them. Strangely, too—especially for Gaine with his personal recollection of government tampering with a free press— the authorities made no effort to muzzle the newspapers, although they chafed at what they considered seditious writings. Lieutenant Governor Cadwallader Colden of New York damned the press, which, he said, "by the most daring inflammatory Papers without the least regard to Truth or public decency excited the Minds of the People to such a highth [*sic*] that they thought their natural Liberty was in the greatest danger." [9] Indeed, wrote the lieutenant governor to his superiors in London, the people were "disturbed excited & encouraged to Revolt against the Government, to subvert the Constitution & trample on the Laws," by the newspapers. [10] Agitated as he was, however, Colden determined that "this is not a proper time to prosecute the Printers & Publishers of the Seditious Papers. The Attorney General likewise told me that he does not think himself safe to commence any such Prosecutions." [11]

In the summer of 1765, leaders in the colonies sought to capitalize on the bonds of colonial unity which opposition to the Stamp Act had created. On July 15, Gaine reported in the *Mercury* that colonial leaders were making plans for a Stamp Act Congress to be held in New York in October, which would present the British government with a united America's objections to the act. He indicated that he was in full sympathy with the aims of the Congress; he carried news of the preparations and stated that he "hoped neither the Governor of Virginia or any other Governor on the continent, will think this so improper a step as to dissolve their assemblies to prevent it." It was, he said, "the right of subjects to petition the King and Parliament fit for the redress of grievances."

Throughout the rest of the summer, Gaine printed notices that committees were being formed in various colonies to correspond with each other in preparation for the Congress. But after the delegates convened in October, he was strangely silent on their activities; he noted only their names, that they had begun deliberations, and that their work was "the most important that ever came under Consideration in America." Not until six months later did he print in the *Mercury* the resolutions of the Congress, and these he had copied from an "extraordinary," or specially published, edition of the *Providence Gazette*.[12]

October 28 marked the date of the last edition of Gaine's *Mercury* before the act went into effect, and that edition presented him with a dilemma. Other publishers, he knew, were expressing their opposition to the stamp duties by bordering their newspapers in black or by printing a skull and crossed bones below the nameplate. He must have questioned whether he should not, also, show his displeasure in a similar way. But in the end motivated, perhaps, by his unwillingness to unduly aggravate the royal authorities, he decided merely to suspend publication. As part of the strategy of legal opposition to the tax, businesses closed rather than violate the act, and Gaine told his readers in that last issue:

The Printer of this Paper, returns his hearty Thanks to the Public in general, for the many Favours he has received from them since the 8th of August 1752, that being the Day this MERCURY was first published here; and its universal Reception is the most convincing Proof of its Utility; It must now *cease* for some Time and the Period of its *Resurrection* uncertain; the Reason of which, is too well known to every Individual in AMERICA.—When it is *revived,* the Printer hopes they may depend upon being well served, and upon as easy Terms as by any other in the Province. He also requests all those in Arrear for the MERCURY, that they would pay off what they owe as soon as possible; likewise, all Persons indebted for Books, Stationary, Advertisements, &c, discharging their Accounts, will much oblige

> Their very Humble Servant,
> H. GAINE [13]

Gaine abruptly changed plans, however; the Sons of Liberty had resolved that the presses of the city would keep operating.

These militants posted a general warning to printers to continue business as usual, and as reinforcement, sent the printers individual notes. Gaine undoubtedly received a letter similar to one sent to John Holt which urged that the editor of the *Weekly Post-Boy* "not be deterred from continuing your useful Paper, by groundless Fear of the Detestable Stamp-Act." Otherwise, he was told, "should you at this critical Time, shut up the Press, and basely desert us, depend upon it, your House, Person and Effects, will be in imminent Danger; We shall therefore, expect your Paper on Thursday as usual; if not, on Thursday Evening—C A R E." [14]

Gaine probably realized that the Sons of Liberty meant exactly what they said. He was not alone; Lieutenant Governor Colden, whose house was ransacked by them on November 1, described them later as so savage "that no Man must speak his sentiments without danger to his Person and Effects." [15] And if Colden was biased in his appraisal because of his position, Gaine's old master, the crusty patriot James Parker, was not. Writing to Benjamin Franklin, Parker spoke of "the Dread every one is Under of Opening their Mouths against [the Sons of Liberty]." [16] Nevertheless, Gaine had marched arm in arm with the radicals to this point and really needed no intimidation; he had fought the Stamp Act quite as strongly at Holt and even more forcefully than Weyman. There would be no rest at the print shop, Stamp Act or no Stamp Act.

On Monday November 4 a news sheet printed at Gaine's shop in Hanover Square was circulated in the city as usual. In place of the familiar nameplate, however, the sheet bore the legend "No Stamped Paper to be Had." Another appeared on the following Monday, and on the Monday after that, November 18, still another. The uproar against the act was so great, and so timidly did the royal officials react, that Gaine felt secure in reinstating the *New-York Mercury* nameplate with the issue of November 25— and without the hated stamps. His name, however, did not appear on the newspaper until the next issue, December 2, and then at the bottom of the last column of news; but it was restored to its place in the nameplate with the issue of December 9.

Gaine also supported a movement to open all other businesses. On December 2, 1765, he carefully reported a protest "Meeting of about Twelve Hundred Freemen and Freeholders of the City of New-York" which "put Business in Motion again in the usual Channels without Stamps" and sent a mild protest to the General Assembly. In it, they requested the legislators to present the "Claims, and the Grievances of the Country" to king and Parliament and that "all necessary Relief [be] prayed for, and sollicited [*sic*] by proper Agents, in the most respectful and constitutional manner;" but Gaine favored even stronger action. "We apprehend that in Cases of such Moment, the plainest and strongest Expressions are best," he wrote petulantly in a rare editorial comment. Gaine reiterated his support of a petition, defeated by the meeting, which called on the legislature to sanction "transacting Business as usual without Stamps" and suggested that "as this is the Session in which the Salaries of the different Officers of Government are settled, we expect that you will make it a Condition, that no officer shall be entitled to any Salary, who refuses to discharge the Functions of his Office, on unstamped Paper."

Gaine and the other colonials continued their agitation against the Stamp Act through the winter of 1765. Meanwhile, the British government of George Grenville fell, and the official movement for repeal of the measure began. On September 23, 1765, Gaine published a letter from London in which the writer stated that it was the opinion of many in official circles that the act would be suspended and that under the new ministry "would be eased many of the Burthens" the colonists bore. Similar assurances of repeal followed. When news came that the American reaction to the act had been sharply felt in England, Gaine issued an "extraordinary" edition of the *Mercury* on February 20, 1766. He reported in it that all the English newspapers had carried news of the American grievances, and wrote: "It is said People at Home universally approve of their Proceedings respecting their Opposition to the Taxation; only the Destruction of Private Property they condemn." How significant Gaine's comment on the violence of the Sons of

Liberty would be in explaining his position on future issues, not even Gaine himself could have known then.

In the next months, Gaine kept his readers informed of developments in Parliament, where the situation in America had become the most pressing order of business. Then in early April came the first hints that the Stamp Act had been repealed. Gaine was hopeful that the reports were true; nevertheless, he put a caveat on the news: "Altho' we doubt not that it is really repealed, yet we cannot assure our Readers that these Intelligences are a Confirmation thereof; but hope soon, very soon, to have a more Direct Account." [17] Later in the month, on April 26, two letters with more direct accounts arrived from London within hours of each other. The first told that a bill for repeal had been introduced into Parliament; the other reported that the House of Commons had passed the repeal bill and that it was to go to the House of Lords for final legislative action. Gaine did not wait to print them in the *Mercury;* instead he had them set in type and distributed both on a broadside.

By May 12, Gaine could tell his readers that there was "not the least Room to doubt that the Stamp-Act is long ago repeal'd; So that there appears at present no Occasion for any further Exertion of ourselves against it." But he used a different kind of medium in the middle of the month when official news came, first of the repeal, and then of the king's assent. Both called for broadsides to be printed and distributed.

The first came on Friday May 16. Gaine printed the text of the repeal act, along with that of the concurrent Declaratory Act by which Parliament hoped to save face in the colonies—the reaffirmation of its "full power and authority to make laws and statutes of sufficient force and validity to bind the colonies and people of America, subjects of the Crown of Great-Britain, in all cases whatsoever."

The following Tuesday, May 20, the New York docks erupted in turmoil when John Hancock's brig *Harrison* sailed into the harbor in mid-afternoon with a copy of the March 18 *London*

Gazette aboard. The newspaper carried the information that the king had given his assent to repeal. Gaine put the news in the hands of a compositor. He told the workman to ready it for publication in a broadside and to title it "Joy to AMERICA!" Confirmation of the report came from Philadelphia at five o'clock that evening, while the compositor was still at his task, and Gaine ordered him to include that information in a note at the bottom of the sheet.

For weeks after, Gaine's *Mercury* carried news of the celebrations which attended repeal. In Boston, Philadelphia, and New York, and in lesser towns and villages throughout the colonies, the *Mercury* reported, the colonists tolled church bells, fired guns into the air, held banquets, and drank numerous toasts. Repeal brought renewed loyalty to the mother country, and expressions of fealty to the king were coupled with salutes and toasts. New York made plans to erect statues of George III and William Pitt, who had championed America's cause in Parliament. It was a heady time—perhaps, too much so. Forgotten in the uproar was the fact that the Sugar Act still stood; and no notice was taken of the ominous Declaratory Act.

During the Stamp Act crisis, the *Mercury,* like the other colonial newspapers, had changed significantly. Physically, it was little different from what it had been at the beginning of the decade. Editorially, however, Gaine had replaced its bland fare of literary, religious, and scientific writings with more important political tracts. Even in relatively minor matters he was less hesitant in expressing his own attitudes. For example, when the Reverend George Whitefield left New York in early 1764, tired after seven weeks of preaching there, Gaine had commented:

May God restore this great and good Man (in whom the Gentlemen, the Christian, and accomplished Orator shine forth with such peculiar Lustre) to a perfect State of Health, and continue him along a Blessing to the World and the Church of Christ.[18]

Or, on a civic matter, Gaine sounded more like an editorialist of a century or two later:

That it may get to the Magistrates of this City.—Several of our Customers desire us to mention, that in the most dark and Stormy Nights, when Lamps are most Necessary, they are the latest and worst lighted, and sometimes not at all, and particularly last Wednesday Night, when there was hardly any passing without Light, and there was scarce any Lamp lighted in the City.[19]

More important, he had begun to focus attention on American events and issues rather than on news from Britain. In so doing, he was helping foster that strange and visionary idea of an American future which the Reverend Burnaby had observed and, in the process, was making the *Mercury* an influential organ of public opinion.

The Sons of Liberty and other patriot leaders would have had to consider Gaine an ally. As the patriot poet Freneau conceded in having Gaine describe those days:

> I first was a Whig with an honest intent;
> Not a fellow among them talked louder or bolder, . . .

But despite Gaine's forthright opposition to the Stamp Act, the Sons of Liberty saw a firmer ally in John Holt, publisher of Parker's *Weekly Post-Boy*. After repeal, they offered to finance Holt in setting up a new newspaper; in October 1766 Holt accepted the offer, ended his partnership with Parker, and began publishing the *Journal, or General Advertiser.*[20]

Parker resumed full control of the *Weekly Post-Boy* on Holt's departure; but, with Holt the darling of the radical element, the *Weekly Post-Boy* would never again be financially sound, and within ten years it ceased publication. Competition for the favor of the radicals proved disastrous even sooner for William Weyman, for he was forced to discontinue his *Gazette* the next year.[21]

Holt's venture did not harm Gaine financially but it helped to determine the political complexion of the *Mercury* in disputes with Britain which were still to come. Just ahead were new duties imposed by Parliament—the Townshend Acts. Once again the colonials would counter with essays and a nonimportation agreement; Gaine could not compete with Holt in presenting the militant position, but neither could he fully support the conservatives. Choosing, instead, a middle course, he seemed to vacillate between the two extremes.

CHAPTER 7

Fair Liberty's Call

New Yorkers must have pursued their amusements with more gaiety than usual in the summer following repeal of the Stamp Act. They enjoyed fishing on the two rivers which bounded their island; or, parties of thirty or forty gentlemen and their ladies would drive to country homes along the East River in their Italian chaises once or twice a week, dine on turtle, drink tea in the afternoon, and fish or play at cards until returning home early in the evening. That winter, the dances at their balls must have been more sprightly and the laughter on their sleighing expeditions a little louder.

Gaine had little political news to print to disturb their good humor. Taking advantage of the respite himself, he completed the second volume of the *Journal of the Votes and Proceedings of the General Assembly of the Colony of New York, 1692–1765*, which he had begun in 1762; the first volume had appeared in 1764. He also printed in 1766 and 1767 his usual variety of almanacs and sermons, George Fisher's *The American Instructor; or, Young Man's Best Companion*, Solomon Gesner's *The Death of Abel*, in five volumes, and *A Complete Introduction to the Latin Tongue*, by Robert Ross.

The lull, however, was brief. The Rockingham ministry, which had repealed the Stamp Act, fell, and Lord Chatham, William Pitt, came to power. Unaware of the turmoil the appointment would bring, Gaine noted in the *Mercury* on September 29, 1766, that Charles Townshend had been named Chancellor of the Exchequer in Chatham's cabinet. While New Yorkers danced in the winter of 1766–67, Townshend was devising a new plan for taxing America. In legislation which Parliament passed the following summer, duties were placed on wine, oil, lead, glass, paper, painter's colors, and tea. The taxes were not burdensome, but the methods of enforcement were onerous. British commissioners, appointed by the king and independent of local control, would collect the duties, and they were given a powerful weapon to help them in their task: writs of assistance, expressly legalized, allowed searching of any home or warehouse where smuggled goods might be kept. Legal action against those who evaded the duties would be carried out by Admiralty courts.

Readers of the *Mercury* were forewarned of the new duties in a short item which appeared on April 13, 1767. But not knowing quite what to expect, the writers who had assaulted the Stamp Act were all but silent. Two essays touching on the undercurrent of disaffection between Britain and America appeared in the *Mercury* in May, however. Both of them were distinctly conservative in tone and gave readers a foretaste of arguments which Gaine later advocated wholeheartedly. The first, reprinted on May 11 from the *London Gazetteer* of March 5, was entitled: "RIGHT, WRONG and REASONABLE, according to AMERICAN IDEAS, and the genuine Meaning of certain MANUSCRIPTS Lately imported." The writer was unsympathetic to American demands that trade restrictions on the colonies be eased. He stressed that, according to the colonists' view, it was right for Britain to aid America, but wrong for her to demand anything in return. And it was reasonable that America be allowed to increase her coffers by trading with Europe while denying her commerce to Great Britain. Such views, the writer intimated, were patently absurd.

The second of the essays, signed by "Populus" and reprinted

from the *Boston Gazette* of Benjamin Edes and John Gill, appeared a week later on May 18. "Populus" argued that "Enemies of Great-Britain and her Colonies" were trying to force the two apart. He implored the colonists to show that "they are as one Man, to support the Crown and Dignity of His most sacred Majesty, and the Authority and Rights of Parliament, and of the General Assembly, upon the well known and established principles of the British Constitution." That such sentiments could have come from Boston is surprising in view of that city's thunder-and-lightning opposition to the Stamp Act, but in the aftermath of that controversy, Boston conservatives made themselves heard as they had not earlier. Possibly to counteract this influence, Gaine printed on May 25 an item stating that a pamphlet was being distributed in Boston "which contains many letters wrote [*sic*] by the favourers of the late stamp-act in America." The printer noted, however, that these "cannot give any pleasure to a real friend to his country, as they contain more falshood [*sic*], malice and ill-will towards America than even a B——d was ever suspected for."

Months later, on October 19, Gaine published an essay by another conservative who argued that Americans should henceforth be more moderate in their relations with the British. Calling himself "A True Patriot," the writer asked: "Can they be so blindly led away with political enthusiasm as not to perceive their inability to oppose the mother country?" In the next issue, October 26, Gaine opened his columns to the radicals. He allowed "Libermoriturius" space to reply that the colonists could deal with Great Britain only from a position of power and that it was necessary to show the ministry what power they could wield. Such sentiments, however, came infrequently; it was apparent that the printer preferred a return to the days when there was calm under the Crown.

Gaine's attitude changed only after copies of the Townshend Acts arrived in America. He printed both the schedule of duties and the texts of the Acts;[1] reading them, he realized they were still another knot in Britain's fiscal leash on the colonies. And when the eloquent John Dickinson began circulating his "Letters from a Farmer in Pennsylvania to the Inhabitants of the British Colonies" arguing against the measures, Gaine printed them. He published the first of the letters, which had appeared originally in the *Pennsylvania Gazette,* in the *Mercury* of December 3, 1767, and continued them through the issue of March 7, 1768.

He must have noticed the subtle difference between Dickinson's arguments and those put forth in the Stamp Act days. Then, the colonists had argued that the internal or excise taxes which the stamp law imposed were illegal. Townshend, while disavowing any distinction between internal and external taxes, had confined the new legislation to tariff duties—external taxes. Dickinson, in his essays, also rejected the distinction; but Gaine could note that he drew a new one between taxation for the regulation of trade and taxation to raise revenue. Parliament, Dickinson argued, could impose the former, but only colonial legislatures could enact revenue measures; the Townshend Acts, then, were also illegal.

The "Pennsylvania Farmer" was appearing in the *Mercury* when Gaine became public printer of the province of New York in January, 1768. He replaced William Weyman, who had held the post since 1759. Weyman had secured it from James Parker—somewhat deviously, according to Parker—when he dissolved his partnership with Parker and began publishing the *Gazette.* By 1767, however, Weyman was hopelessly in debt. He had little foresight and was unable to estimate his costs properly; neither was he successful in collecting his accounts; and he was dishonestly lax in paying his own debts. Two days before Christmas in 1767, he published the final issue of the *Gazette,* and almost immediately afterwards, with creditors hounding him, he came to Gaine. Would Gaine buy his public printing contract? He would ask only one year's receipts from the post.[2]

Considering his competitor's predicament, Gaine must have thought it a stroke of good fortune which had kept Weyman from accepting the offer of a partnership fourteen years earlier; but the Irishman could also pity the hapless Weyman. But Gaine would not have dwelt long on reminiscence or pity. Even without paper

and pencil, Gaine could calculate the benefits. Weyman owed him
about £300; would that not cover the payment of a year's receipts,
so that he would have only to tear up Weyman's note to have the
position? [3] More important, the post of public printer, like that of
postmaster, was a profitable form of governmental subsidy for the
colonial printer, providing both financial reward and social status.
Gaine told Weyman he would take the contract. All that remained,
then, was to submit the agreement to the General Assembly for
ratification.

Weyman's skills as a printer were on a par with his bookkeeping
abilities. The Assembly in 1766 had reprimanded him for careless
workmanship, while Gaine had won their approval with his edition
of their votes and proceedings.[4] The two-volume work had been
carefully executed, and that by itself would have been enough to
recommend him. But politics was just as important to the conservative assemblymen. Parker wanted to be reinstated, but the
DeLancey faction recalled only too well his display of independence
in publishing Presbyterian tracts in the fight over the college fifteen years earlier. The DeLanceys remembered, too, that Gaine had
shown allegiance to them in the past, and they rewarded him by
ratifying his agreement with Weyman; [5] they would not be dis-
appointed in his future performance.

To denote his official position, Gaine changed the name of his
newspaper on February 1, 1768, to the *New-York Gazette; and the
Weekly Mercury.* He removed the figure of Mercury, which had
appeared in the center of the nameplate for a little over four years,
and replaced it with the coat of arms of the province. But, as he
admired the effect of these changes on the *Mercury's* appearance,
Gaine might well have paused to consider the peculiar problem
his prestigious position posed for him: as a member of the Establishment and as a newspaper publisher, he must serve the government and, at the same time, avoid antagonizing the enemies of
government. It is doubtful, however, that Gaine saw the consequences which would follow this feat of political tightrope-walking.

Gaine was paid by the Assembly for each official document he

published; he could pocket the profits derived from public sales of
the volumes; and his position brought him other printing orders.
Sir William Johnson, the king's Superintendent of Indian Affairs,
contracted with Gaine later in 1768 to print a prayer book in an
Indian language.[6] Weyman, who had started the work in 1763, had
been a bad choice. He lacked the necessary fonts of type to complete the job; he worked slowly; and he made frequent errors in
the text. When he died some five months after resigning as public
printer, the work was still incomplete. Once again, Gaine showed
his skill as a printer. Given the job in July, he finished the printing the following February and sent the books to the bindery.[7] The
speed with which he was able to accomplish this task indicated
that he was not only conscientious, as usual, but that he also must
have added at least one press and a greater variety of type to his
shop.

Proof that the Assembly had made a politically wise choice came
with the outbreak of another episode in New York's political-
religious turmoil. Late in 1767, John Ewer, bishop of Landaff,
preached a sermon before the Society for the Propagation of the
Gospel in which he referred disparagingly to what he considered
to be the decayed state of religion in the colonies. He called Americans infidels and barbarians, and suggested that an Anglican episcopate be established in the colonies to oversee their religious practice.[8]

The suggestion renewed fears of the dissenting sects that the
Church of England once more was attempting to become the established church in the colonies. The sermon drew an immediate
response from William Livingston, who wrote as "The American
Whig" in James Parker's *New York Gazette: or Weekly Post-Boy*
of March 14, 1768. Livingston enlisted the aid of Smith and Scott,
his colleagues of the 1752–53 college controversy, and together
the triumvirate kept up their essay assault in the *Weekly Post-Boy*
through July 24, 1769.

Four Church of England divines, Samuel Seabury, Charles
Inglis, John Vardill, and Myles Cooper, styling themselves "Tim-

othy Tickle, Esq.," flailed the opposition with "A Whip for the American Whig" in the *Mercury* from April 4, 1768 to July 10, 1769. This time, Gaine upheld only the conservative Anglican position. The printer opened the columns of the *Mercury* to the Presbyterians only once, when he allowed "Pro Patria," to state their case briefly. But that essay was followed by a rebuttal from "Pro Artis," who discredited "Pro Patria" by saying the latter "was employed *by* the Faction to do their dirty work; and I am *sure* that *Pro Patria* is a *very proper instrument.*" [9]

The triumvirate fared better than they had a decade earlier; the British ministry feared that the establishment of a colonial episcopacy would aggravate an already dangerous situation and dropped the idea. Of greater significance, the triumvirate had given added impetus to the impulse for independence. John Adams noted half a century later: "The objection was not merely to the office of a bishop, though even that was dreaded, but to the authority of parliament, on which it must be founded." [10] And rejection of parliamentary authority was at the very heart of the revolution. Gaine, however, had shown that he was not willing to reject that authority.

Meanwhile, Dickinson's "Pennsylvania Farmer" letters had spurred the colonists to action against the Townshend Acts. Recalling their victory in the Stamp Act crisis, they hoped to beard the British lion once again, and "fires of opposition and resistance" [11] began to blaze throughout America. One of the first manifestations of the new opposition was another nonimportation movement which spread through the colonies in the winter of 1767–68. It, too, won Gaine's support in the *Mercury*. For example, when Newport, Rhode Island, agreed on a nonimportation compact in December, a newspaper writer exhorted the colonies: "Save your Money and save your Country! ought to be echoed throughout the whole continent." Gaine echoed his words by reprinting them in the *Mercury* of December 28, 1767. Typical of the many other items on the same theme which appeared in the *Mercury* during the period was an article, reprinted from a Philadelphia newspaper, that assured readers that nonimportation "cannot if now agreed upon by us, fail of obtaining a speedy and effectual Relief from this Grievance." [12]

But the colonists lacked the unity they had during the Stamp Act crisis, and each group seemed to wait on the other before taking firm steps. In April, the New York merchants agreed not to import any goods from Britain after October 1, 1768, "provided the Merchants of Philadelphia and Boston come into the same Measures." Finally, the news came from Boston that merchants and traders there "unanimously voted not to send any further Orders for Goods to be ship'd this Fall, and that from the 1st of January 1769, to the 1st of January 1770, they will not send for or Import either on their own account or Commissions, or purchase of any factor or others who may import any Kind of Goods or Merchandise from Great Britain," with the exception of "Articles necessary to carry on the Fishery." [13] Almost immediately, on September 12, 1768, Gaine was able to tell his readers that merchants in New York had met and signed a similar pledge.

New York's tradesmen gave added strength to the movement by resolving not to buy or use any merchandise that was imported contrary to the agreement made by the merchants and traders. They announced they would consider "Persons who shall refuse to unite in the Common Cause, as acting the part of an Enemy to the true Interest of Great Britain, and her Colonies, and consequently not deserving the Patronage of Merchants or Mechanics." [14] They expressed their new unity in song:

> Come, join Hand in Hand, brave AMERICANS all,
> And rouse your bold Hearts at fair LIBERTY's Call;
> No *tyrannous Acts* shall suppress your *just Claim*,
> Or stain with *Dishonor* AMERICA's Name.
>
> In FREEDOM we're born, and in FREEDOM we'll live,
> Our Purses are ready,
> Steady, Friends, Steady,
> Not as SLAVES, but as FREEMEN, our Money we'll give.[15]

There is no evidence that Gaine signed the merchants' agreement; but he evidently sided with the signers. He published letters in the *Mercury* urging the colonists to "avoid every luxury, tho' ever so sweet, till you convince your enemies how difficult it must be, either to enslave you, or drive you to disobedience." [16] As they had during the previous nonimportation movement, the columns of the *Mercury* carried suggestions for strengthening the American economy, such as the establishment of a bank and loan office or the making of wine in the colonies. Again, Gaine singled out for mention those who excelled in home manufactures, such as the family of Ebenezer Hurd of Connecticut, who produced "no less than 500 Yards of Linen and Woollen, the whole of the Wooll [sic] and Flax of his o[w]n raising," and "a Woman that lived in good Fashion; in the Town of Sunderland, in the Western Part of this Province [who] was endow'd with such noble spirit of Freedom, Liberty and Frugality, that she entirely laid aside all Foreign Goods, especially Cloths of a Foreign Manufacture, and cloathed herself in Cloth of her own Manufacturing from Head to Toe." [17]

The publisher gave the Sons of Liberty space in the *Mercury* to announce their meetings and helped them to coerce the population into adherence to the nonimportation agreements. For example, to a letter published July 3, 1769, which warned that outlawed goods intended for Philadelphia and New York were bound for Maryland and would be smuggled into those cities, Gaine appended the comment: *"We shall keep a good Look-out for these Goods."* Gaine also allowed the Sons of Liberty space to make public the names of those who did not live up to the agreement— names, he said, which were to be "transmitted to Posterity with Infamy, in the Annals of their Country." [18]

Gaine further supported nonimportation by publishing pleas urging the less steadfast to adhere to the agreement. "A.B.," for example, argued that nothing "short of an effectual Redress of our Grievances should be intimated as sufficient to justify the Execution of a single Order from hence." [19] A writer in the issue of April 13, 1769, explained that if Britain and America were to have a

"Trial of Strength . . . it may be as well done now as at any other Time."

Such pleas were not always effective. The printer Alexander Robertson, who with his brother James established the *New-York Chronicle* in May 1769, ordered goods from Philadelphia to stock his shop. Called to task, he advertised in the *Mercury* that he had sent the goods back; but it was discovered that he had first uncrated the supplies and sent back only empty containers. On June 21, 1769, an unsigned broadside circulated in the town charging him with "a high Crime and Misdemeanor against the Liberties of the People" and urging that he be regarded as "an Enemy to his Country." Two days later, Robertson issued a broadside in which he apologized and begged "leave to implore the Pardon of the Publick, assuring them that I am truly sorry for the Part I have acted. . . ."

Gaine, too, had few scruples about breaking the agreements, despite his editorial position. When Sir William Johnson asked him, in the fall of 1768, to supply a gilt quarto Bible, Gaine told him that there was not one "in the City to be sold, but I shall endeavour to get you one by the Spring, if I should run it by way of Falmouth, as we have all agreed not to send for any Goods this Winter." Later, however, as the penalties imposed on those who refused to honor the agreements became more apparent, Gaine appeared more timid. In April of the following year he told Sir William that he could not secure a dictionary and other items the official wanted, "but shall send to London for them as soon as we are permitted to import any Goods from that Part of the World." [20] His former employer, James Parker, suspected Gaine and two other booksellers of importing books while the agreements were in force in order to have available stock at the moment importation was once again allowed. Writing to Benjamin Franklin in 1770, Parker predicted: "I imagine there will be large Assortments [of books] sent for by [Garrat] Noel, [James] Rivington and Gaine, as soon as Importations are allowed: — Indeed they have great Parcels here already stored, which they are not allowed to sell, until the Importation takes place." [21]

As we shall see, Parker was only partially correct in his judgment. All three printers did have books stored, but only Rivington and Noel sent orders to Britain as soon as a group of New York merchants, acting on their own, abrogated the nonimportation agreement. Gaine withheld further orders until the agreement officially expired. Nevertheless, Parker could not be blamed if he considered Gaine wholly motivated by profit as, indeed, Gaine appeared to be in breaking the nonimportation agreement. The old patriot had felt what he considered Gaine's disloyalty in 1752, when the Irishman left his employ to start the *Mercury*. Seeing Gaine switch allegiance for no other reason than money in the dispute over the college a decade later, Parker may have concluded that his former journeyman was no more committed to principle than to individuals. Parker would not live to find his suspicions confirmed; but others who may have begun to have similar doubts about Gaine would.

In the meantime, the legislatures of the several colonies began petitioning England for relief from the yoke of taxation. The Massachusetts House of Representatives led the way. Early in 1768 it asked the king and his ministers to ease the burden and sent a circular letter to the other colonial legislatures urging their unified support. The letter stated in cautious terms that Parliament had no authority to lay duties on America merely for the raising of revenue and that the colonies would never be adequately represented in Parliament. Indeed, the Massachusetts men questioned whether Americans could ever really be free while subject to officials appointed by the crown.[22]

Gaine, watching the progress of the letter from the vantage point of his print shop, noticed that the other colonies were reacting positively. Other legislative petitions asking the home government for relief began arriving at the Bible and Crown, and Gaine printed these in the *Mercury* throughout the spring and summer of 1769. When word came that Parliament took offense at the petitions rather than honoring them, he reprinted from the *Maryland Gazette* an essay by "Atticus," who flatly condemned Parliament:

The infamous arts and misrepresentations of a few men in office, actuated by the basest motives of private interest, and ambition, have had greater weight, than the humble and dutiful petitions and remonstrances of all the colonies, and the cries of four millions of loyal subjects.[23]

By daring to print such a letter, Gaine was aligning himself, at least for the moment, more firmly with the militants. He did, in fact, print similar essays whose arguments were designed to reinforce and strengthen the colonial resolve to resist the new duties. But there were fewer of these than in 1764 and 1765; he was still printing the "Whip for the American Whig" series for the "Timothy Tickle" group and it continued to run in the *Mercury* until midsummer. The "Whip" essays filled nearly a full page of each issue, and sometimes more, leaving him little space for other lengthy writings.

At last, the ministry, feeling the pinch of nonimportation, heard the petitions and the remonstrances. It was not long before Gaine would print an optimistic observation from a man in London: "The storm is gathering very fast about the m— —try—the nation calls loudly for a change—they begin to feel the effects of nonimportation. . . . If the colonies prove steady and firm, the late acts will be repealed." [24] When Parliament met in January 1770, it was confronted with the American problem. Within the session, the Townshend duties, except for the tax on tea, were repealed effective December 1.

During the crisis, Gaine, now forty-three, had been courting Cornelia Wallace, a thirty-five-year-old widow. On September 6, 1769, the two were married at Trinity Church by one of the *Mercury*'s "Timothy Tickle, Esq." essayists, the Reverend Charles Inglis. Nothing is known about Cornelia before her marriage to Gaine; but she must have brought new warmth to the printer and his three small children: eight-year-old Elizabeth; John, seven; and Anne, just nine days shy of her fifth birthday, who had never known her real mother.

At about this same time, Gaine was reevaluating his attitude toward the nonimportation agreement. He was among those who knew that nonimportation was an effective political weapon. He also knew that it was sapping his resources and, as we have seen, he did not accept financial sacrifices easily. With his business growing, he had been importing from England an increasing number of books, fine paper and writing materials, and pills and ointments. He would need additional shipments of those goods if he were to continue to prosper.

Other merchants felt as Gaine did. Unkempt and always rushed, the printer had heard the grumbling about the restrictions of the agreement as he made his rounds of the *Mercury*'s advertisers and subscribers. John Waddell, leaning on the counter in front of a depleted stock of sailcloth, shoes, and soap—all British-made— wondered how long he could stay in business if he could not replenish his shelves with imports. The same problem confronted Thomas Forsey as he looked around at his stock of fabrics, snuff, and drinking glasses, and Gerardus Duyckinck, who owned the largest general store in the city and depended heavily on British goods to stock it. Duyckinck was mightily pleased with the fancy advertisements of scrollwork and line-by-line listing of goods which he and Gaine had devised for the *Mercury,* and he did not want those lists to shrink in size.

Waddell, Forsey, and Duyckinck were only a few of the many merchants who soon began agitating for an end to the agreement. A group in Boston sent Nathaniel Rogers to New York "to use his Endeavours to prevail on the Merchants there to break through and put an end to their Agreement." Rogers might have been successful, but the Sons of Liberty persuaded him to leave town lest he be "visited in a more disagreeable Manner." [25] The Sons of Liberty and other more militant New Yorkers were determined that the agreement should stand until the Townshend duty on tea also had been repealed. Believing they had widespread support, the militants polled the merchants. The results, which Gaine displayed on the first page of the *Mercury* of June 18, 1770, showed the opposite:

New Yorkers stood by their pledge to import no tea or other goods from Great Britain "upon which a Duty is laid or hereafter may be laid, for the Purpose of raising a Revenue in America," but they wanted to begin importing other items on December 1, the day repeal of the Townshend Acts was effective.

The New York merchants nevertheless hesitated to act alone, and they appointed a committee to seek concurrence of their counterparts in Boston and Philadelphia. Boston and Philadelphia rejected the proposal and received support for their steadfastness from Connecticut and New Jersey, both of which resolved to carry on no trade with New York if she abrogated the agreement. Undoubtedly thinking of his pocketbook, Gaine commented almost wistfully on July 9, "the Non-Importation Agreement remains in full force, and doubtless will continue so, till the End is obtain'd."

New York's merchants needed trade with England more than trade with the other colonies, however, and about eight hundred of them agreed to abrogate even without the support of their fellow colonists. On Wednesday, July 11, when the packet boat *Earl of Halifax* sailed out of New York harbor bound for Falmouth, she carried orders "from the Merchants here for a general Importation of Goods, except the single Article, TEA." [26]

Gaine appeared to be in full sympathy with the importers. In reporting their decision to import, he referred to those who wished to maintain the agreement as "the opposite Party!" In subsequent issues of the *Mercury,* he published letters deriding the decision to reopen trade,[27] but the majority of the essays he published on the subject reflected a belief that the colonies should avoid antagonizing Britain. These latter stressed the financial benefits to be obtained from a thriving free trade. In their eagerness to justify abrogation, some writers even assumed the mantle of patriotism, as did "Veritas," who claimed in an essay on September 3, that New York's decision to import showed that "none have *acted up* to what they professed, with more *Integrity,* than the Merchants of New-York; while *those* of Boston are remarkable *only* for practicing *less* and professing *more* than all the rest of the Continent."

Although Gaine published such sentiments, he did not immediately send an order for books, as did his competitors James Rivington and Garrat Noel. On November 19, both Rivington and Noel
advertised stocks of newly imported books. Because Gaine did not
advertise a new list of imports until February 11, 1771, he probably
had not sent orders until after December 1, the terminal date of the
nonimportation agreement.

Like Rivington and Noel, however, Gaine had stored stocks of
books which he advertised in the *Mercury* of July 9. Until the
agreement ended, he subsisted on sales of these books and sales of
books he published himself. The latter included *The Oeconomy of
Human Life*, "Translated from an Indian Manuscript, written by an
ancient Bramin [*sic*]," and *The Child's New Play-Thing*, "Being a
Spelling-Book, intended to make the learning to read a Diversion
instead of a Task." In early October, Gaine published *Hutchin's
Improved Almanac*, and the next month, the *New-York Pocket
Almanac*.

But while the output of his press seemed to remain much the
same as it had been in earlier days, the printer was a changed man.
He had grown weary of the financial setbacks resulting from the
policies of the radicals; he was even more repelled by the violent
tactics of those who tried to force acquiescence to those policies.

CHAPTER 8

Most Shocking Transactions

In the late summer and early autumn of 1768, Gaine had complemented his more militant journalistic stand against the Townshend Acts with reporting of British reprisals against Boston for Massachusetts' role in leading opposition to the legislation. The circular letter of the Massachusetts House of Representatives had alarmed the British government. Lord Hillsborough, secretary of state for North American affairs, sent urgent instructions to the colonial governors in which he termed the circular letter an attempt "to excite and encourage an open Opposition to and Denial of the Authority of Parliament, and to subvert the true principles of the Constitution."[1] He ordered the governors to exert their utmost influence to defeat what he called "this flagitious Attempt to disturb the publick Peace." When Governor Bernard of Massachusetts received these instructions in the summer of 1768, he ordered the House to withdraw the circular letter; when they refused, he dissolved the assembly.[2]

Gaine sympathized with the Bostonians in the beginning; he also knew the value of a good news story. As a result of Hillsborough's instructions and Bernard's action in implementing them, Boston became a tinderbox of discontent, and Gaine focused his readers' attention on every subsequent event which might spark an ex-

plosion: Britain's plan to quarter troops there; the formation of a
Committee of Convention to protest the plan; the committee's
petitions to Governor Bernard to recall the Assembly, and the
arrival of the troops and their quartering on the Common and in
Faneuil Hall.[3] Reports came to the Bible and Crown in exchange
newspapers from Boston, and Gaine was kept busy clipping them
for reprinting in the *Mercury*.

In October 1768 Samuel Adams, leader of Boston's opposition
to Britain, and his followers began circulating to newspapers in the
colonies what they called a "Journal of Occurrences," a daily
chronicle of alleged British encroachments on the freedom of
Bostonians. John Holt published the first in the series in his *New-
York Journal* of October 13, 1768. Not to be outdone, Gaine reprinted it in the *Mercury* of October 24, but gave it the title
"Journal of the Times." On November 7 he reprinted another in
the series and entitled it "Journal of Transactions." Holt continued
publishing the "Journal" in his newspaper until November 20,
1769; Parker also carried it during that year in his *Weekly Post-
Boy*. But after the November date, Gaine not only printed no more
of the news notes, but he also sharply reduced the amount of such
news from Boston. Readers who relied solely on the *Mercury* were
not informed of the increasingly more volatile situation in the
Massachusetts capital. Instead, the "Boston" column contained only
stories of official government activities there and items describing
such everyday events as robberies and fires.

Perhaps Gaine believed that he did not need to report events
which were being so thoroughly covered by his competitors. Moreover, the "Whip for the American Whig" essays, already discussed,
were still filling the *Mercury*'s pages. Considering Gaine's imminent
shift to conservatism, it is also likely that he suspected Bostonians
were provoking Britain at a time when they should have been
trying to eliminate the causes of friction with the mother country.
In aggravating Britain, Boston could expect only more reprisals,
and these might be extended to other cities in the colonies as well.

Gaine became all the more disenchanted with the lion-baiting activities of the New Englanders early in the new year. On February 6, 1769, he reprinted from a Boston newspaper a letter, purportedly from London, which stated that Governor Bernard of Massachusetts was "to have a pension on the American establishment of £2000 paid out of revenue, raised by a tax on your lawyers, clerks of towns and courts." Furthermore, Lieutenant Governor Thomas Hutchinson was to be promoted to governor "with a fixed sallary [*sic*] of £1500 per annum, to be paid out of a revenue raised on your American woollen manufactures." Gaine later learned that he had been tricked; the letter was a forgery. He would have something to say to his readers about that.

As he sat down to write, he knew he could not out and out condemn the Bostonians who had perpetrated the hoax. Instead, he was careful to note that "the performances of many of the real Writers from England, who contrary to the fundamental Principles of the English Constitution, audaciously presume to claim a Right to plunder their American Brethren of their Liberty and Property, are sufficiently remarkable for their Impudence and Stupidity." Then he came to the heart of the matter: "yet we have reason to believe, that some of the most impudent and senseless that have appear'd in America, as Extracts of Letters from England, were fabricated by some . . ." He may have paused: "persons?" Was that the word? Much too mild. Anyone who would commit such a forgery with the sole aim of driving a wedge between the mother country and her colonies was nothing less than a traitor. And so he wrote: ". . . fabricated by some Traitors on this side of the Water." The ink blotted, Gaine handed the scrap of paper to the compositor to be set in type for the issue of February 20. That would take care of the Bostonians for now; but he would be more careful about what he printed in the future.

A year later, in reporting the Boston "massacre," Gaine was wary of radical representations of the incident. The first reports he printed in the *Mercury* expressed the radicals' view: "This most shocking Transaction alarmed the People,—the Bells were set a ringing—and all the inhabitants that were able, assembled at the Place where the

Murder was committed." [4] However, Gaine soon began to express conservative reaction. In an "Extract of a Letter from Boston," dated March 19, 1770, and printed in the *Mercury* of April 2, an unnamed correspondent said that he found it necessary "to shew that the People of this Town, have not upon all Occasions, been so innocent, and so free from Aggression, as they represent themselves." On the arrival of the troops at the place where the mob assembled on the evening of the incident, "the lower sort of People, whose Minds were poisoned to that End, instead of looking on the Soldiery as fellow Subjects, and Countrymen, they viewed them with the malignant Eye of Detestation, and Insult, as a mercenary Banditti, in the Hands of most benevolent Majesty, ready to perpetuate every Act of Devastation and Cruelty." The mob "fully intended to attack a sentry," and when Captain Preston, the squad leader, sent out a sergeant and twelve men, the mob struck them and shouted insults at them. One of the soldiers, after being hit, had fired, and the others had discharged their weapons in confusion.

On December 17, Gaine published a conservative's view of the trial of the soldiers involved. Justice was done, the writer contended, because the jury found two soldiers guilty of only manslaughter and the other six not guilty. The writer attributed the outcome to the fact that no Bostonians were on the jury, only people from the surrounding countryside who were "not under such strong Prejudices" as Bostonians. "Indeed," he observed, "from the Borders of Connecticut all the way to Boston, you will find People in every Town exclaiming against Boston, for imposing upon the Country by false Representations, and drawing them into Measures which they say will ruin the Province; in Boston itself, many who were very high say they have gone too far." It must have been obvious to his readers that Gaine was beginning to share these sentiments, not merely superficially because of the position he held, but out of the conviction that Boston could ruin the other colonies, as well.

In reporting political disturbances in New York, Gaine apparently hesitated to offend the provincial government. On at least one occasion, he printed the official version of an incident. After a crowd led by the Sons of Liberty had rampaged through the streets on the night of November 14, 1768, Gaine printed a letter from Augustus Van Cortlandt, the town clerk, describing what took place, "as Mr. [John] Holt's Representation of it may deceive Persons at a Distance"; Holt's report, of course, was highly favorable to the Sons of Liberty.[5] The authorities had deliberately chosen the public printer to relate their account, Governor Henry Moore asking the mayor of the city to secure "a Counter Represtn [*sic*] in Gaine's Paper." [6]

Moreover, Gaine was not unwilling to serve the government beyond the requirements of his official duties. In the 1770 session of the General Assembly, for example, the radical party attempted unsuccessfully to pass a bill requiring the election of assemblymen by secret ballot. Gaine sided with the conservative DeLanceys in opposing the effort. To him, as well as to "A Number of Gentlemen . . . the independent Freeholders and Freemen" of the city, whose petition to the legislature to oppose the measure he printed in the *Mercury*, the secret ballot would oblige the electorate to choose their representatives "in a secret and clandestine Manner." As such, it would be a surrender of their privilege of "declaring our Sentiments openly on all Occasions." In short, declared the conservatives in this and other petitions and essays which appeared in the *Mercury*, the secret ballot was a "dangerous innovation, directly contrary to the old Laws and Customs of the Realm, and unknown in any royal British Government on the Continent." [7]

Basic to the conservative argument, of course, was a mistrust of the mob. As has been shown, the conservatives had begun to recoil from the tactics of the Sons of Liberty, who recruited most of their members from the lower classes. Even the moderates were being alienated by the radicals' "fondness for *bawling out the word freedom, and sporting with liberty colours, liberty caps, and liberty poles, which no more become men than the tops, marbles, paper kites, and other play things of children,*" [8] and by the use of these symbols to excuse their violence.

The "liberty colours, liberty caps, and liberty poles" served also
to annoy the British soldiers garrisoned at Fort George, at the tip of
Manhattan Island. The liberty pole, especially, became a target for
their abuse. The Sons of Liberty had erected one, a tall mast set in
the common grounds, in 1766 "in commemoration of the Repeal of
the Stamp-Act, the Triumph of Constitutional Liberty over the Attempts of arbitrary Power to destroy it; and as a Monument of
Gratitude to his Majesty, and the British Parliament who repealed
the Act, and to those worthy Patriots, both in and out of Parliament, by whose Influence the repeal was obtain'd." [9] The Sons of
Liberty came to regard the pole with almost sacred awe; at the
same time, the British troops made it an object of derision. It was
not long before the two groups were brawling in the streets.

As Gaine could easily have observed, the life of the British soldier
at Fort George was anything but exciting. As is true of foreign
garrison duty in modern armies, it was a dull routine of polishing
leather, and shining brass, of standing inspections and walking
guard duty, close-order drill and full-dress ceremonials, and of a
myriad other plodding tasks. Many of his duties were designed
simply to occupy his time. Once off duty, the soldier relieved the
loneliness of being an ocean away from home and the boredom of
the barracks with the only pleasures his low pay could afford:
drinking, easy women, and fighting. It was not surprising, then,
that a group of redcoats, perhaps spurred by too much rum and the
ribaldry of an evening at a bawdy house, might reel toward the
commons to torment the Sons of Liberty by attacking their revered
liberty pole.

The first such incident occurred on August 10, 1766. A corporal
and a regimental drum major led a handful of men from the
Twenty-eighth Regiment to cut down the pole. A number of New
Yorkers, undoubtedly Sons of Liberty, signed depositions later that
the attack was meant to be an "insult to the Town," and angered,
they planned revenge. As Gaine pieced together the story for his
report in the *Mercury* of August 18, there resulted "two Frays
between the Town People and the Soldiers, a small Number of

each, in which two or three were wounded, and several hurt, by the Soldiers." The soldiers who destroyed the pole were jailed, and their officers promised to court martial or to hand over to civil authorities others found guilty of subsequent "misbehaviour." Gaine had no personal comment on the incident; possibly he believed that the officers' promise would dissuade other soldiers from further provocations. But the British troops were not so easily discouraged.

Another group attacked the pole in October. Armed with bayonets, they had first gone, Gaine reported on October 27, "to several houses in the Fields, where they were noisy and abusive, to the great disturbance and terror of the inhabitants. This was occasioned, it is said, by ill-treatment which some of the Soldiers had received the night before, at some of those infamous houses, which to the great scandal of our wholesome laws are suffered to exist as so many receptacles for loose and disorderly People."

Soldiers destroyed the pole again on the evening of March 18, 1767, after a Sons of Liberty celebration commemorating repeal of the Stamp Act. Gaine once again reported the affair and took the opportunity to show his annoyance with the soldiers: such efforts to "offend and insult" the citizens of New York must not occur again, he editorialized. But the troops were to cut down the pole twice more in the next three years.

In January 1770 the Sons of Liberty erected what they thought was an indestructible liberty pole: a sturdy wooden mast, covered with iron bars riveted and hooped nearly to the top and secured in a deep hole. It took the redcoats three successive days of assaults before they finally brought it down.

By this time, mob hatred of the British was at a peak. The constant attacks on the liberty pole, the military occupation of Boston, the loudly proclaimed distress over the Townshend Acts all served to kindle emotions. On January 18, two days after the "indestructible" pole was downed, the Sons of Liberty captured some soldiers who were posting handbills denouncing the Americans and dragged the redcoats to the office of the mayor. Twenty other men from the garrison hurried to the rescue while a crowd of Americans gathered to back up the Sons of Liberty. Fearful of trouble, the mayor ordered the troops to return to their barracks, but on their way they were attacked from all sides by outraged New Yorkers. Fists and makeshift weapons flew until officers from the fort appeared and herded the soldiers back to their quarters.[10] That was the Battle of Golden Hill; the first blood-spilling of the Revolution had taken place on the streets of New York a full month before the Boston Massacre.

Gaine, as might have been expected, did not immediately publish the news. But neither of his Whig rivals, Parker and Holt, publicized it immediately, either; however, the New York Sons of Liberty did not enjoy the leadership of a powerful and imaginative Sam Adams, as their Boston comrades did, and they apparently failed to realize the propaganda opportunity the battle provided.

Parker finally did give an account of the incident in the *Weekly Post-Boy* of February 5, but it was unbiased and couched in cautious and innocuous terms. An anonymous letter describing the battle from the point of view of the Sons of Liberty then appeared in Holt's *Journal* "for the satisfaction of such of your Customers as take your Paper only." Inexplicably, Gaine reprinted the same letter in the *Mercury*.

In an attempt to prevent further disorders, the common council of the city voted nine to six on February 2 not to allow the erection of another liberty pole on the common grounds. The Sons of Liberty then bought a small plot of land and raised a new pole, one that was to stand until it was cut down during the British occupation of the city six years later. They bought a house near it, the Corner House on Broadway, where they could meet and plot their activities and keep watch over their embattled totem.

As in the Stamp Act days, the Sons of Liberty also kept close watch on printers. As they sat in their new meeting rooms in the Corner House, they may have puzzled over Gaine's attitude toward them and their activities. Some probably argued that Gaine supported them. Had he not held the soldiers responsible for the recent clashes? And had he not, like their good friend John Holt, printed the radical account of the Golden Hill incident? Others could have argued, with more confidence, that Gaine opposed them. He had printed conservative accounts of events in Boston. Moreover, he was being paid by the government and he had not only ignored some of their propaganda efforts because he knew the government would not want the incidents publicized, but he also had printed an official version of the disturbance of November 1768.

That Gaine was leaning toward the conservative position was obvious. However, careful readers of the *Mercury* could point out another aspect of the printer's position: despite his own quick temper, Gaine would not condone violence by anyone, either the friends of government or its enemies; and he may have feared that publicizing the "propaganda of the fist" would only lead to more bloodshed, as it had in Boston. Those readers could have predicted, also, that as the Sons of Liberty grew more wanton, Gaine's opposition to them would become more pronounced.

The long years of discord between the Sons of Liberty and the British soldiers produced a deep-seated bitterness between the two groups; and when the Assembly, in its 1770 session, granted funds to provision the garrison at Fort George, the Sons of Liberty were infuriated. Within weeks after the Battle of Golden Hill, a handbill castigating the legislators for their action appeared on the streets of New York. The handbill, addressed "To the Betrayed Inhabitants of New York," charged that the Assembly "have not been attentive to the Liberties of the Continent nor to the Property of the good People of this Colony, in particular. We must therefore attribute this Sacrifice of the public Interest, to some corrupt Source." [11]

The handbill had been printed at James Parker's shop, and one of his workmen, Michael Cummins, pointed to Alexander McDougall as the author. McDougall, a leader of the Sons of Liberty, was arrested and charged with seditious libel. To the Whigs, McDougall immediately became a hero to be compared with England's John Wilkes. Wilkes's Number 45 of the *North Briton,* which reported some of the proceedings of the House of Commons, had resulted in his arrest for sedition; and the Whigs, seizing on another symbol of official tyranny, added "45" to their litany of patriotism. Then on February 14 "the Forty-fifth day of the Year, forty-five Gentlemen, real Enemies to internal Taxation, by, or in Obedience to external Authority, and cordial Friends to Capt. M'Dougall, and the glorious Cause of American Liberty," called on McDougall in his jail cell. There they dined with the prisoner on forty-five pounds of steak, cut from a forty-five month old bullock, and afterwards drank forty-five toasts "expressive not only of the most ondissembled [sic] Loyalty, but of the Warmest Attachment to Liberty, its renowned Advocates in Great-Britain and America, and the Freedom of the Press." [12]

To the conservatives, McDougall was not a hero but "a principal promoter and encourager of the unhappy disputes which raged with such violence in the colony," [13] and they turned to the *Mercury* in their efforts to discountenance both the imprisoned "American Wilkes" and his followers. In contrast to Parker, who published extracts from Andrew Hamilton's defense of John Peter Zenger in support of McDougall,[14] Gaine printed "The Dougliad," a series of essays expressing the conservative view, which ran in the *Mercury* from April 9 through June 25. The unknown author or authors of the series sarcastically excoriated McDougall, defended the Assembly, and looked to the English common law of libel as justification for McDougall's imprisonment.

Freedom of the press must be checked, "The Dougliad" contended in the April 23 issue. "If there was no check to Malice and Falsehood, Government must soon sink into Contempt, and the subject be stript of Protection." McDougall's handbill was an outstanding example of the kinds of writing which held government up to contempt. "Not even the pen of a junius [sic] could have contrived an essay, better calculated, to blind and seduce, to distract and disunite, to foment discontent, tumults and sedition; and in short to trample down all legal authority, and shake the government to the foundation," the "Dougliad's" author charged. The *ad hominem* argument was the series' principal weapon:

It it not justifiable to display him [McDougall] in a contemptible Light; who, setting no bounds to his own vindictive Spirit, has boldly charged the most eminent and amiable Members of the Community, with the detestable crimes of Corruption, Perfidy, and Parricide?

The Assemblymen did not merit McDougall's attack, the author of one of the essays in the series wrote, because they simply "did their duty, and consulted the State, and true Interest of the Colony." [15]

True as ever to his policy of neutrality in all such controversies, Gaine stood ready to make his press available to McDougall for a reply should the imprisoned Son of Liberty "think himself injured by any Thing that may be inserted in this Paper." [16] Other supporters of McDougall may have taken up the challenge, but Gaine printed the offerings of only two of them—and neither made a straightforward defense of his hero. "The New-York Satyrist," who wrote two essays, attacked the conservatives as those "in favour of old Times and arbitrary Tory-Measures, and the unmerciful, accursed STAR-CHAMBER TORY-DOCTRINES," and derided the English common law of libel as "arbitrary STAR-CHAMBER LAW." "Hoadly," the second of the two writers, was more restrained. He wrote only two short letters taking issue with minor statements made in "The Dougliad." [17]

Gaine made one other effort to placate the Sons of Liberty. On May 7, he reprinted in a column of news from Boston a letter which had been sent to Benjamin Edes and John Gill, publishers of the *Boston Gazette,* and which urged them not to hire Cummins, the workman who had revealed Parker as the printer of the "Betrayed Inhabitants" handbill. Cummins, the letter read, was a "vile miscreant" and a "Sordid Harpy," and the writer hoped that "Printers who are friends to liberty, will treat him on application to them, as he deserves; and that they will reprint this description of him, for the information of the Public."

The McDougall case was never finally decided. McDougall was indicted by a grand jury, but he was not taken before the petit jury because of the death of Parker, who was to have been the chief

witness against him. But the case left a breach in relations between
the conservative and Whig factions which could not be healed.[18]
Replying in the *Mercury* of April 9 to a tract which had appeared
in Holt's *Journal,* "Philoclerus" drew the distinction from a conservative position:

I am glad [the author] honours the Friends of Peace, Order, Government, and constitutional Liberty, with the Appellation of *Tories.*
If those who are for throwing every Thing into Confusion, and make
Liberty to consist in doing whatever a Man pleases, tho' to the Injury
of others—of which he has given a notable Sample—If those I say,
assume the name of Whigs, it is the readiest Way to bring a Word,
harmless and unmeaning enough in itself into thorough Contempt.

From that time forward, it was obvious that the New York conservatives were determined that an aristocratic few should govern
the province and that opposition to Britain should be led by men
who held "Peace, Order, Government, and Constitutional Liberty"
in higher esteem than did the Sons of Liberty, and Gaine apparently
shared their views. If the writings which appeared in the *Mercury*
actually reflect his attitudes at this time, he believed that the mob
must be controlled and that violence was not the way to accomplish
redress of grievances.

That Gaine should have held such opinions, besides merely
promulgating them for the sake of economic survival, is understandable. He was no longer merely a tradesman, but the proprietor of a large printing establishment. He jealously guarded his
investment against oppressive governmental economic policies, but
he was also opposed to violence of any kind and his growing
wealth bred a fear of the vengeful mob. A mob grown too powerful could become more dangerous than the government. Moreover, he was public printer and he had certain responsibilities to
the government he served. All of these factors influenced Gaine
at the midpoint of the revolutionary movement; they would ultimately lead him to loyalism.

Within the print shop, other concerns drew Gaine's attention.
Both his apprentices and journeymen were posing more problems

than ever before. Perhaps it was the disjointedness of the times, but as James Parker observed "the present race of young Printers seeming to me most of them, so abandoned to Liquor, as to deserve little Encouragement, besides, their Honesty should be tried first." [19] Gaine, like his fellow printers, knew that apprentices were restless; he had endured the difficulties of apprenticeship himself. Usually in their teens, apprentices rose early, between five and six o'clock, to start the heating fires and to prepare the shop for the day's work; at night, they were made to read proof until midnight or, during the printing of long works, even later. In return, they received only their education in the trade, a bed, ordinary food, and a small allowance for clothing. Because of these conditions it was difficult to obtain apprentices and difficult to keep them. Benjamin Franklin and Parker, among others, had fled their masters rather than endure the hardships demanded of them, and later apprentices emulated them, always to the master's anger. Gaine probably sputtered with rage as he dashed off an advertisement for the return of one runaway:

Run-away from the Subscriber about 12 o'clock Yesterday, an Apprentice Lad, named Daniel Narraway: He is about 5 Feet 6 Inches high, well made, pretty much pitted with the Small-Pox, wears his own Hair and is very much bloated by Drinking, to which he is most addicted: Had on when he went away, a brown Coat, Jacket and Breeches, Shoes and Stockings, but no Buckles in his Shoes, having lately sold them, and spent the Money: He is supposed to be lying drunk in some petty Tavern in the OutWard of the City, or gone up to New-England. Whoever takes up the said Lad, so that he may be lodged in the Work-House, shall have a Reward of Five Dollars, paid by

H. GAINE

N.B. All Masters of Vessels are forbid to carry him off at their Peril; and whoever harbours him after the Date of this Advertisement, shall be prosecuted as the Law directs in such Cases. This is the second time he has run away in about a Month.[20]

Another of Gaine's apprentices tried his hand at counterfeiting theater tickets in what little spare time he had and distributed them

to fellow apprentices. The counterfeits came to light when Lewis
Jones, one of Parker's apprentices, tried to use them. Because the
ornamentation on them was similar to that on the originals, which
had been printed at Gaine's shop, Gaine was questioned about
them. He, according to Parker, "was so base, as to suppose they
might be done at my House," and animosity between the two publishers developed further. Jones, in fact, at first said that Parker's
son Samuel had given them to him. Later, however, Jones "clear'd
Sammy, and own'd he had them of Gaine's Lad." [21]

Journeyman printers of the period were generally an itinerant
and unreliable bunch; the same Lewis Jones is a good example.
After he had completed his apprenticeship with Parker, Jones
worked as a journeyman in the printing shop of Alexander and
James Robertson before securing employment with Gaine. Still
later, he was accused of counterfeiting money. Brought to trial, he
was acquitted only through the intervention of Parker; Parker's
son had visited Jones's family in England and had been well-
treated by them, and the father felt obligated to repay their hospitality by acting as a character witness for Jones. Subsequently,
Jones fled to South Carolina.[22] Other printers were little better,
and while Gaine might advertise for compositors and pressmen who
were, like himself, "sober and diligent," he had to be content with
disreputables like Jones.

New faces had appeared on the New York publishing scene
during the long months of crisis. As already noted, the two
Robertsons, who had employed Jones, had started their *New-York
Chronicle* in May 1769, but the newspaper lasted only eight months
and died in January 1770. Parker had a low opinion of the two
brothers and their newspaper, and in a letter to Benjamin Franklin,
he described them as "two Scots Paper Spoilers" who "puff'd and
flourish'd away a While" before ceasing publication and going to
work for the bookseller James Rivington, who was turning his
hand at publishing books.[23] However, they would be more successful at publishing a newspaper during the British occupation seven
years later.

A great loss was that of Parker. His death on July 2, 1770, removed one of the most enterprising of New York's printers and one of the pioneers of printing in that colony, New Jersey, and Connecticut. As has been noted, Parker traced his roots to William Bradford, whom he had served as an apprentice. Later, he had been in partnership in several ventures with Franklin. Although Gaine had considered himself slighted by Parker in 1752, and despite their subsequent personal and political differences, the *Mercury's* publisher praised his former master in an obituary. Parker, Gaine truthfully—and, perhaps, enviously—wrote, "was eminent in his Profession. He possessed sound Judgment, and an extensive Knowledge: He was industrious in Business, upright in his Dealings, charitable to the Distressed." [24]

Parker's son, Samuel Parker, published the *Weekly Post-Boy* for a few weeks after his father's death, but he leased it early the next month to Samuel Inslee and Anthony Car. Inslee and Car continued the newspaper beginning with the issue of August 13, but they would not be serious competition for Gaine.

John Holt was now Gaine's major rival. On establishing his *Journal* in 1766, he had made it the unofficial organ of the Sons of Liberty, and the Whig element continued giving him its support. Since then, the *Journal* and the *Mercury* had provided New York readers with a slight diversity of opinion. But strong or weak, radical or conservative, the newspapers of New York all showed one marked similarity. All were devoting more space to American affairs and American ideas, and even their different viewpoints were distinctly American. As such, they were both reflecting the changing character of colonial thought and helping to solidify the colonials' view of themselves as a community separate from Britain.

Three years of relative calm followed repeal of the Townshend duties. Then came passage of an act giving a monopoly on tea exports to the British East India Company. Until then, Gaine all but ignored politics; but from that time onward, like it or not, he and the *Mercury* would be inextricably bound up in the politics of revolution.

CHAPTER 9

Tea, but No Sympathy

🙥 Between 1770 and 1773, Hugh Gaine's *New-York Mercury* appeared remarkably similar to the *Mercury* of the 1750s. Sam Adams and the other Whig propagandists tried in vain to keep discontent alive in the colonies, but Gaine, like most other printers, refused to aid them. Instead, he filled the *Mercury* with everyday news, much of it in the category of human interest, such as a tale he printed on March 15, 1773:

> Some Time past, as a certain Man was crossing Hudson's-River, between New-York and Albany, on the Ice, having in his Hand a Bottle of the good Creature, he fell in Bottle and all, but fortunately got out again; when, missing his Bottle, he like a resolute Hero, boldly ventured his Life, by diving after the same, which he got, and safely took it home to Regale his Spirits with. A rare Instance of Courage and Love to the Juice of the Vine. However unaccountable this may appear, it is a Fact, and can be prov'd by several that saw it acted.

Similar whimsical items came from the London newspapers, as did this bit of court gossip reprinted in the *Mercury* of August 30, 1773:

> A certain noble Lady notoriously known for infidelity, being told that adultery, in a woman among a tribe of Indians on the continent

of America, was punished by obliging the woman to lay with different men until she expired, replied, "then I heartily wish adultery was transportation in this kingdom, that I might to and reside with so *well judging* a body of people."

While these and items like them were appearing in his newspaper, Gaine could reflect with satisfaction on his twenty years as a publisher and the affluence the *Mercury* was bringing him. As he began his third decade of publishing, the printer had gathered sufficient profits to invest in real estate. In 1770 he bought 6,000 acres of land in Albany County which had been owned by a former governor of the colony, William Cosby, and later that year he was one of sixteen purchasers of former governor George Banyar's estate. In 1774, in partnership with Henry Onderdonk and Henry Remsen, he established "at a very great expense" [1] a paper mill at Hempstead, Long Island, an undertaking which was later described as "one of the most notable enterprises of the late colonial period" in New York.[2]

New Yorkers could not have been surprised at Hugh Gaine's increasing affluence. His frugality was well known. Had he not, as Freneau was to observe, "neglected [his] person, and looked like a fright" on the streets as well as in the print shop? His fellow townspeople snickered even more about his tightness with money. They gossiped that he would never give a note in payment for goods or services, but always paid cash. They liked to tell about the man who bet that he could hoodwink Gaine into a debt. He approached the printer, they said, and offered him some goods at a low price, but only on condition that Gaine give a note in payment. Never one to pass up a bargain, Gaine accepted, and the bettor went to bed that night thinking he had won the wager. Then came a knock on the door, and there stood Gaine, money in hand. He had to pay the note, the printer said, because he had never before given one and he could not sleep for worrying about it.[3]

Gaine aspired to more than wealth, however; he wanted social position as well. Two principal elements dominated New York society during the period. On the one side, assertive tradesmen and mechanics, the lifeblood of the Sons of Liberty, struggled to impose democracy on their country that they might have a voice in its government. Arrayed against them was an embryo aristocracy which modeled itself on that of England. Its members were either families whose claim to superiority had roots in the mother country or families of more humble origins who had been "able to work their way to the top of the social ladder by industry, shrewdness, and good fortune after their arrival in America." [4] Gaine had reached at least the lowest rungs of the latter group.

When he married Cornelia in 1769, he had listed his occupation as "Stationer," as if the mere title could raise him out of the class of tradesmen and mechanics to which other printers belonged. He sent his son John to preparatory school at Mr. Haddon's in Newark, and in 1774 he would enroll the youth at King's College, where the boy would be a classmate of Alexander Hamilton.

Gaine also was active in the affairs of the community. Still a member of the Grand Provincial Lodge of the Freemasons, he had later joined the St. Andrew's Society, served as treasurer and vice president of the St. Patrick's Society, was a vestryman of Trinity Church, and sat on the board of governors of the city's hospital. Surveying his twenty years as publisher of the *Mercury,* he could take pride in his accomplishments. It was satisfying for a man to realize that he had used his abilities to a most profitable advantage and that he had the respect of his peers.

Gaine's family had increased by two during the calm. The date has been lost, but Elizabeth, his first child, was about ten, her brother John, a year younger, and Anne, seven, when Cornelia presented the printer with a third daughter, whom they also named Cornelia. In 1772, another daughter was born and named Sarah, after Gaine's first wife. In Cornelia and Sarah, Gaine would see his hopes for social position fully realized.

As the 1770s began, Gaine had competition for the town's newspaper readership from only John Holt and his *Journal* and from Samuel Inslee's and Anthony Car's fading *Weekly Post-Boy.* But in the spring of 1773, Gaine's principal competitor as a bookseller, James Rivington, began publishing *Rivington's New-York Gazetteer; or the Connecticut, New-Jersey, Hudson's River, and Quebec Weekly Advertiser*.[5] It will be recalled that Gaine and Rivington apparently had little in common when the latter arrived in New York in 1760 to start his bookstore. Now, however, the former London dandy and the one-time Belfast apprentice shared a conservative outlook in politics. Gaine found, too, undoubtedly to his chagrin, that "Jemmy" Rivington, as the new publisher's detractors called him, had a flair for publishing which made his *Gazetteer* one of the most popular newspapers in the colonies. It soon rivaled the *Mercury* in typographical excellence, editorial variety, and conservative tone, and came to pose the most serious competitive threat that Gaine had yet faced. Indeed, Rivington would ultimately take not only some of Gaine's subscribers and advertisers, but also the public printer's position of favor with the government. It is doubtful that Gaine anticipated losing his publishing supremacy; however, he would find that those setbacks would redound to his own advantage.

Gaine reacted without alarm to Rivington's appearance as a newspaper publisher. Now sitting between the political poles represented by Rivington and the radical Holt, Gaine retained a slight conservative leaning; but he saw the best course to follow would be to make the *Mercury* the journalistic voice of moderation in New York. Certainly, he could find more comfort in a moderate rather than extreme political position; he would not seriously alienate either conservatives or radicals. Neither, however, would his moderation fully satisfy either side.

The immediate result of Rivington's entrance into the newspaper business was the disappearance of James Parker's old *Weekly Post-Boy*, which had already been seriously damaged by the success of Holt's *Journal*. Inslee and Car published the *Weekly Post-Boy* until August 13, 1773, when they relinquished their lease to the owner, Parker's son Samuel. Parker and his partner, John Anderson, tried to revive it, but they, too, were unsuccessful; in the fall of 1773, after thirty-one years of publication, the newspaper ceased publication.[6]

The two-year hiatus in British-American differences came to an abrupt end in the spring of 1773. The easing of tension following the Townsend Acts furor had been accompanied by an increase in business activity in the colony. But its economic recovery was threatened once more with the passage by Parliament in May 1773, of the East India Company Act.

The East India Company, a prime supplier of tea for Britain and her colonies, had fallen into financial chaos and was on the brink of bankruptcy when Parliament came to its aid by giving it a monopoly in the colonial tea trade. It then could export directly to the colonies, rather than first selling to exporters in England, who in turn supplied the American importers who sold to colonial retailers. The act thus eliminated the four profits American consumers had formerly had to pay, and the company's tea could be sold for a much lower price than that charged by American merchants. But while the three-penny Townshend duty on tea was continued, the company was given a full refund of duties on tea imported into England and later shipped to the colonies.[7]

Colonial merchants naturally opposed the measure. Those who smuggled their stocks through Holland—and there were a number of them—hated it because it threatened their lucrative trade. Fair traders who bought their tea legally in London were against it because it gave an English company a monopoly, undercut their own profits, and rendered nonimportation ineffective as a means of opposition.

Gaine published the text of the act on September 6, 1773, but it was not until late October that he printed anything indicating colonial opposition. Then he reported only that a group of citizens had sent a memorial to ship captains and the merchants of London expressing appreciation "for their patriotic Conduct in refusing to take from the East-India Company, on Freight, a Quantity of Tea, on which a Duty laid by the British Parliament was made payable in America on Importation." Although opposition had been slow in asserting itself, its intensity was indicated by a resolution of the same group which stated that "Stamp-Officers and Tea-Commissioners will ever be held in equal estimation." [8]

Gaine, who was not so directly affected by the act as he had been by the Stamp Act and the Townshend Acts, gave only halting support to the resistance movement. He printed little news of its progress, but carried only occasional, isolated items, such as one from Newport printed on November 29, relating that "50 or 60 families in this town, who have constantly used tea in their houses for a long time, have lately entirely refrained from that pernicious herb; and that numbers of others are on the point of abandoning the disgraceful practice of tea drinking." But, while trying to remain uninvolved, he also felt moved to publish on December 6 an excerpt from a London paper which warned the ministry: "A storm is now gathering in America, which will either ruin the friends and dependents of my Lord Bute in this country, or separate the colonies forever from its dominions."

With storm clouds billowing, the printer reversed course again. A new note of Whig-like militance sounded in his news columns— at least for a time. He also reported on December 6 that the three tea commissioners in New York, Henry White, Abraham Lott, and Benjamin Booth, declined to receive the tea consigned to the city, "there being a general Opposition to the Sale of it, as it stands charged with a Duty payable in the colonies." After Sam Adam's Mohawks had destroyed a consignment of tea aboard the *Dartmouth* in Boston harbor in December, Gaine published a veiled warning that the same action might be taken in New York. He said that he had "the inexpressible Satisfaction" of telling his readers that when the ship *Nancy* arrived with tea, its commander, Captain Lockyer, would be "made acquainted with the Sentiments of the Inhabitants respecting the Shipping that Article, which will indubitably occasion his return with it in *statu quo* to England." [9]

The *Nancy* was turned back without incident, but the Sons of Liberty soon had an opportunity to stage their own tea party on the

ship *London.* As Gaine told the story to his readers in the *Mercury*
of April 25, 1774, the New York committee of observation
boarded the *London* when it arrived in New York three days before, found tea, and informed a mob that stood near the ship. A
special group, called Mohawks after their Boston cousins, "were
prepared to do their Duty at a proper hour," Gaine reported. "But
the Body of the people were so impatient that before it arrived a
Number of them entered the ship, about 8 P.M. took out the Tea,
which was at Hand, broke the Cases and started their Contents in
the River, without doing any Damage to the Ship or Cargo."
Summing up the incident, the printer editorialized in words which
might well have come from a Sons of Liberty propagandist:

Thus to the great mortification of the secret and open Enemies of
America, and the Joy of all the Friends of Liberty and human Nature,
the Union of these Colonies is maintained in a Contest of the utmost
importance to their Safety and Felicity.

Gaine, with his aversion to violence, could not have been edified
by the tea parties; neither could others who believed as he did that
violence would only bring repercussions from Britain. It was not
surprising, then, that while Gaine appeared to be siding with the
Whigs in opposition to the tax, he resumed his antimob stance of
the Townshend Acts period. Describing Gaine's attitude at the
time, Philip Freneau would later have him say:

Well, as I predicted that matters would be—
To the stamp-act succeeded a tax upon Tea:
What chest-fulls were scattered, and trampled, and drowned,
And yet the whole tax was but threepence per pound!
May the hammer of Death on my noodle descend,
And Satan torment me to time without end,
If this was a reason to fly into quarrels,
And feuds that have ruined our manners and morals;
A parson himself might have sworn round the compass,
That folks for a trifle should make such a rumpus.

Gaine opened the columns of the *Mercury* to those who pleaded against violence and counseled for a more moderate course. For example, on May 16, 1774, he printed the suggestion of "A British American," who asked in an essay whether it would not be wise for the Bostonians to raise "a Sum equal to the estimated Value of the DROWNED TEAS . . . with a solemn Declaration (conceived in respectful and conciliating Terms) that they make the Reimbursement with sincere Pleasure, as they thereby have at once an Opportunity of testifying their Readiness to Repair every private Loss that Individuals may sustain in the present unhappy Struggle for the Maintenance of their just Rights." Such a procedure, the writer contended, would declare the Bostonians' continuing patriotic sentiments and, at the same time, "conform to the Requisitions in the Act of Parliament that now threatens their Destruction [the imminent Boston Port Act], as could not fail to place them at once in the light of Constitutionally dutiful Subjects to the Crown." Continued violence, he warned, could only lead to war; and to take arms against the massive British forces would be the maddest possible course.

Another Tory writer, who gave what he called "The Account between Britain and her Colonies candidly stated," argued in the June 6 *Mercury* that America was indebted to Britain for peace and security and for the futherance of her economic well-being; Britain was indebted to America for consumption of British manufactures and for income derived from duties and trade. If the two severed their ties, the results would be disastrous for both:

Without the support of Britain, America must become tributary to some other nation; without America, Britain would cease to be an opulent, powerful nation; their interests are inseparable, and their separation is incompatible with their natural ideas and high notions of liberty and freedom, in the pure and unadulterated sense in which ancient, not modern, patriots have conceived them.

Therefore, he said, America must not only compromise, but acquiesce to Britain on the revenue question.

These and other conservative writings served to moderate revolutionary zeal. But Gaine, perhaps fearing reprisals from the Sons of Liberty, still found it necessary to disclaim an essay, "The Right of the British Legislature to tax the American Colonies," published on May 30. He told his readers that he was printing the piece only that "the Publick may judge of the Arguments made use of by the Mother Country for taxing the Colonies." Nevertheless, Lieutenant Governor Colden was able to write to his superiors that the atmosphere of terror which had gripped New York was abating. "We have no more burning of Effigies, or putting cut throat Papers under People's doors," he said. The conservatives had more leeway to express themselves, and could "now speak & publish Sentiments, in favour of Government, and argue upon the political Subjects of the Times, with much greater freedom & security than has been known here for some years past." He was confident, in fact, that "the licentious Spirit which has governed the People to their great Disgrace, is check'd." [10] But, as future events would show, Colden's optimism was premature.

The situation in Boston remained so violent that Parliament was stirred to impose severe sanctions on that city. On May 16, 1774, Gaine printed the Boston Port Act, a measure which threatened the town's destruction by closing the harbor there to "the landing and discharging, lading or shipping of Goods, Wares, and Merchandise." This was a clear reprisal for the destruction of the *Dartmouth*'s tea. That act was followed by the Administration of Justice Act and the Massachusetts Government Act, and then by the Quartering Act. As a result, Boston became a town under martial law, and other colonial cities grew concerned that Parliament would place legislative clamps on them, as well. Their only recourse, they began to reason, was to unite. Even Gaine could ask editorially: "Should the other colonies continue inactive spectators of the struggles of the Bostonians, when she is sacrificed to ministerial vengeance, then will a similar act be forced upon us?" To reinforce his concern, he chose to print at the same time an essay which carried his reasoning even farther. The writer pointed out that "the teas have been destroyed not at Boston alone, some of them have been thrown overboard at New-York, and the whole sent back from Philadelphia." It was imperative, then, that the other colonials give the Bostonians "every possible and lawful assistance, and encourage them in a justifiable defence of their rights, by the earliest intimation of our readiness to unite with them." [11]

Responding to such exhortations, the merchants of New York met and formed a fifty-man committee of correspondence to discuss with our Sister Colonies upon all Matters of Moment." [12] Gaine was not a member of the committee, but through the late fall and winter of 1774 and 1775, he filled the *Mercury* with similar resolutions from the other colonies expressing their sympathy and unity with the people of Boston. These reports, by stressing common fears and common action, served to bond the colonies together.

Correspondence between the colonies was effective; still more effective would be a meeting between representatives from the various colonies. Gaine printed in the *Mercury* of June 27, 1774, a call from the Massachusetts legislature for a congress "to consult upon the present State of the Colonies," to be held at Philadelphia "or any other Place that shall be judged most suitable," on the first of September 1774. The other colonies responded favorably. Each of them began making preparations to send "Deputations, to assist at a grand Congress of Representatives of all the Colonies,—to whose Wisdom, Firmness, and Fortitude, the Liberty, Property and whole Interest of this free and august Continent are to be delegated."

Gaine apparently favored the plan when it was first proposed, and the *Mercury* reported preparations for the congress in approving tones. However, as delegate selection got under way, it appeared that those who were chosen as representatives favored another boycott of British goods. Some among the colonists, in fact, feared that the delegates might be so rash as to enact measures which would ultimately lead to a break with England and, per-

haps, to war. Gaine evidently shared these fears, for he began to
show hostility to the congress in the pages of the *Mercury*. As he
would be made to say in Freneau's poetical satire:

> [I] still was unwilling with Britain to part—
> I thought to oppose her was foolish and vain,
> I thought she would turn and embrace us again,
> And make us as happy as happy could be,
> By renewing the aera of mild Sixty-Three.

None of the Tory writers in the *Mercury* questioned the right of
the colonists to hold the congress, although one, writing on
August 15, reminded the delegates of their allegiance to Great
Britain and warned them not to "deny the authority of Parliament
where it alone can have jurisdiction." That essayist enunciated a
frequent Tory argument, that Parliament had the right to levy
duties on articles imported by the Americans and that the colonists
should not challenge that right. Indeed, he said, "while we contend
for our rights, let us not attempt to deprive them of theirs." Finally,
he pleaded with the congress not to sever the bond of union with
Great Britain "which has made the empire we belong to so great
and glorious."

Another common argument came from an essayist who pointed
out on August 22 that as British subjects, Americans enjoyed a high
level of prosperity compared to "the Wretchedness of Nine Tenths
of the Globe." If the colonists broke from England, misery would
come to them as well; and immoderate action by the congress
would ultimately bestow "the Rights of Conquest" upon the
mother country. Not even the Whigs, however, were ready to declare independence in 1774.

With cannon salutes and speeches—and with mixed expecta-
tions—New Yorkers saw their delegates to the first Continental
Congress off to Philadelphia at the end of August. As their writers
in the *Mercury* indicated, the Tories sought reconciliation with
Britain at almost any cost; the militant Whigs would not be satisfied with any but stern retaliatory measures. The congress, called
by Whigs, put Whig ideas into motion. Soon after convening, it

resolved that merchants were "not to send to Great Britain any Orders for Goods; and to direct the Execution of all Orders already sent, to be delayed or suspended until the sense of the Congress on the Means to be taken for the Preservation of the Liberties of AMERICA is made public." [13] Those means, Gaine informed his readers in his October 31 issue, included the most stringent boycott of English goods ever undertaken by the colonists. This boycott, which was to take effect the following December 1, was called the Association; and it imposed not only nonimportation regulations, but also decreed strict nonconsumption of British manufactures, and nonexportation of American goods.

While the congress was still meeting, Gaine expressed his displeasure at the prospects of another boycott by publishing two essays by the Reverend Charles Inglis, assistant Rector of Trinity Church. Inglis was not only Gaine's pastor, but his friend. The minister had married Gaine and Cornelia four years before, and he had contributed to the *Mercury* as one of the "Timothy Tickle, Esq." essayists who had produced "A Whip for the American Whig." Later, he would aid in the publication of the *Mercury* in New York while Gaine was in New Jersey. Concerning himself, now, with the preparations for the congress, Inglis styled himself "A New York Freeholder" and declared in an essay Gaine printed on September 19, that "America is now threatened with the calamities of a civil war." Terrified of such a prospect, the minister, in a second essay published on October 10, appealed to conservatives to grasp the reins of leadership in the colonies. Addressing himself to "ALL who have Influence or Property, and are real Friends to the Welfare of this Country," Inglis urged them "to shake off Supineness, and exert their utmost Endeavors to prevent the impending Ruin that threatens us." Undoubtedly, Inglis uttered the same fears from his pulpit and in private conversations with Gaine; as his respectful parishioner, Gaine could not have been uninfluenced by Inglis's arguments.

Nevertheless, although Gaine might not have agreed with the outcome of the congress, he recognized the news value of the proceedings, and on November 28 he published long excerpts of the deliberations of the delegates. He also printed separately a pamphlet which summarized the congress' journals. At the same time, he printed in the *Mercury* numerous expressions of opposition to the Association. Many of these took the tone of a group in Dutchess County, New York, who voted "that we will upon all occasions mutually support each other in the free exercise of our undoubted right to liberty, in eating, drinking, buying, selling, communing and acting what, with whom and as we please, consistent with the laws of God, and the laws of the Land, notwithstanding the association entered into by the Continental Congress to the contrary." [14] Those who objected to the Association failed to realize, however, that the congress had constituted itself a *de facto* legislature, and the measures it adopted would be considered the "laws of the land."

Whig rejoinders to these Tory sentiments came to the print shop, and Gaine fretted over them. He had little sympathy with the writers' views; he did not want to print them. But he had always taken a middle course and he would continue to follow it, even if haltingly. So from time to time he printed the radical works. But the few that he did publish did not satisfy the radicals. The committee of correspondence of Albany cited him by name in a letter warning of "attempts that are daily made by the tools of the Administration to divide us." The *Mercury,* said the committee, was "stuffed with pieces tending to hold up this Province as opposed to the measures recommended by the Congress." The Suffolk County, New York, committee of observation passed a similar resolve. [15] From as far away as Worcester County, Massachusetts, where Isaiah Thomas published his radical Whig *Massachusetts Spy,* came a condemnation of Gaine and four other printers for aiding "the enemies of these united colonies . . . by publishing their scandalous performances in their several newspapers." Gaine might well have worn an ironic smile when he told his compositor to set in type for the February 20, 1775, *Mercury* the committee's recommendation "to the good people of this county not to take any more of the aforesaid papers, but that they encourage those printers who have invariably appeared friendly to this country."

But Gaine's political sins were minor compared to Rivington's.

So steadfastly did Rivington adhere to the Tory line that he was frequently maligned, and no more so than in a broadside addressed to the "Citizens of New York" and distributed on November 16, 1774. The writer left open the question of whether Rivington was "a pensioner from the ministry, or has been influenced by hopes of their future favours." But he was certain "that the general scope and tendency of the news papers published by Mr. Rivington, have been to promote the designs of the British ministry." Rivington would hear stronger, more violent objections the following year.

Gaine, on the other hand, continued to demonstrate the ambivalence which had characterized his editorial performance throughout his career. He tried to secure the approval of both Whigs and Tories. On the one side, he persisted in publishing essays which condemned the proceedings of the Continental Congress as "violent and treasonable" and he argued against sending delegates to a second congress to be held in May 1775. At the same time, he told his readers that "We have the pleasure to hear" that several Long Island towns had elected delegates to the New York provincial congress which was to elect representatives to the second continental gathering.[16] While continuing to print news of scattered resistance to the Association, Gaine joined with a group of other merchants in advertising that a shipment of goods ordered from England before nonimportation went into effect would be sold at a public auction because the merchants were "heartily desirous to comply with the association." [17] It is doubtful that Gaine fooled any readers of that advertisement into believing that he actually wanted to comply with the provisions of the Association; more than likely the Sons of Liberty persuaded him to sell the goods at auction.

Gaine's position in those days of turmoil was, once more, a curious one and seemingly inexplicable. Other printers were committing themselves to one side or the other. Holt, of course, was wholeheartedly Whig and Rivington almost immediately proved to be more Tory than many of the staunchest conservatives. In contrast, Gaine was successfully avoiding such a decision. The time would soon come, however, when he would have to take his stand as a devoted Whig or a full-fledged Tory.

CHAPTER 10

Drums, Fifes, and Propaganda
–American Manufacture

ᔓ The businessmen and merchants who had organized the Sons of Liberty in opposition to the Stamp Act had tried to maintain control of the opposition movement, but by 1775 they knew they had failed. Radicals had taken over leadership positions and America was primed for revolution—a revolution which began with an exchange of gunfire between British soldiers and American militia on the common grounds at Lexington, Massachusetts, on the morning of April 19.

The echo from the shot heard 'round the world reached New York within days. Lieutenant Governor Cadwallader Colden received the official British army report of the Lexington skirmish and the one that had followed it at Concord from General Thomas Gage, the commander at Boston. Colden sent it to Gaine and asked him to publish it. If anyone asked, the printer inquired, could he tell where he got the report? Certainly, Colden told him, and that seemed to settle the matter. Gaine agreed to print it. By the next day, however, Gaine had changed his mind; he would not publish it after all.[1]

Why he had changed his mind, Gaine would not say; but Colden surmised. John Hancock and Samuel Adams, those two hotheads from Massachusetts, were in town and they undoubtedly

94

had put pressure on the printer. Indeed, Colden wrote to Gage, the American rebels were "determined to suppress every account but their own." [2]

Whether he had not returned the official British account to Colden or whether Colden again had asked that it be printed is not known. But Gaine did publish it in June. As always, he worried over what the Whig faction might think, however, and decided he must explain why he was printing it: it had "already been published in several of the Southern Papers," and for that reason could do no harm. Yet he was careful to add, "For the provincial account of the above unhappy Affair, see several of our Papers." [3] That account, published in the *Mercury* of April 24, 1775, read:

Watertown, Wednesday Morning, near 10 o'Clock. To all Friends of American Liberty, let it be known,

That this Morning before Break of Day, a Brigade consisting of about 1000 or 1200 Men, landed at Phip's Farm, at Cambridge, and Marched to Lexington, where they found a Company of our Colony Militia in Arms, upon whom they fired without any provocation, and killed 6 Men and wounded 4 others.

First reports from the battlefield were sparse. Gaine put them on the inside pages and used the front page for a report on Parliament's consideration of colonial petitions for redress of grievances. Thus, although he told the war news from the Whig point of view, he did not display it prominently. It should be noted, however, that the front page was ordinarily made up and printed earlier in the week, and the inside pages printed later; or, as Gaine told advertisers who came in on Sunday night and expected their notices to be placed on the front or back pages, "the first Page of the News Paper is worked off some Times on Friday, and never later than Saturday." [4] Because, as we have seen, the type was hand set and pages had to be hung to dry after printing on one side, it would have been a laborious and costly process to reset and reprint the front page.

More accounts of the Battle came to Gaine during the following

week, and in the May 1 issue of the *Mercury* he devoted more
prominent space to more detailed stories. With them he printed a
letter from Massachusetts, half plea and half threat, urging New
Yorkers to stand beside the New Englanders. "The Eyes of America
are on New-York," read the unsigned letter. Even though the
British ministry believed that New York would side with the
mother country, the colonials had "more than Men enough to
block up the Enemy at Boston; and if we are like to fall by
Treachery, by Heaven, we will not fall unrevenged on the
Traitors" who might desert to the enemy. The writer added:

It is no Time now to dally, or be merely neutral, he that is not for us,
is against us, and ought to feel the first of our Resentment. You must
now declare most explicitly, one way or the other; that we may know
whether we are to go to Boston or New-York; if you desert, our Men
will as chearfully [*sic*] attack New-York as Boston, for we can but
perish, and that we are determined upon, or be free.

Gaine decided he would no longer "dally, or be merely neutral."
Privately, he contributed £30 to the Commercial Association of
New York to help meet that commerce-supporting group's debt of
nearly £3605.[5] Publicly, he placed the *Mercury* squarely in the
American ranks for the first time since the Stamp Act crisis. The
items he printed were as propagandistic as they were informative.
In Freneau's words:

> . . . like a cruel, undutiful son,
> Who evil returns for the good to be done,
> To gain a mere trifle, a shilling or so
> I printed some treason for Philip Freneau
> Some damnable poems reflecting on Gage
> The King and his Council, and writ with such rage,
> So full of invective, and loaded with spleen,
> So sneeringly smart, and so hellishly keen,
> That, at least in the judgment of half our wise men,
> Alecto herself put the nib to his pen.

Gaine's reports from the battlefields carried a tacit Whig imprimatur. On May 15, 1775, after provincial troops from Connecticut captured the British garrisons at Crown Point and Fort Ticonderoga, Gaine printed a one-sided account in which his correspondent editorialized: "The Martial Spirit diffused through this Province at this Juncture is almost beyond Conception." A week later, on May 22, in commenting on scattered action in Massachusetts, the printer added a note of his own: "The public Spirit, Prudence, and enterprising Genius of the New-Englanders, will ever be admired." In each succeeding report from the American army, Gaine editorially lauded the patriots' cause, loyalty, and skill as soldiers. His tone was such that his readers had no reason to doubt his patriotism.

Gaine also attempted to erode British morale, a task made easier because of the opposition to the war by a large segment of the British population. He reported on July 3 that protesters appeared at the embarkation of a troop ship and distributed to America-bound soldiers a broadside which claimed that, in fighting in the colonies, the men would be compelling their "fellow subjects there to submit to POPERY and SLAVERY." In the same issue, he printed letters from two British officers who had resigned their commissions on grounds that they would not help to deprive Americans of their liberties.

Using propaganda tactics he would employ against the Americans a little more than a year later, Gaine sought to exploit British losses. For example: "We hear a Number of Officers Ladies, have lately arrived at Boston, from England, Ireland, &c. and on their Landing they were to a woman, Widows." A favorite device was the publication of letters intercepted from the enemy, particularly letters which hinted at divisions in the ranks. Still another, was the printing of items which told of redcoat discomforts occasioned by supply shortages: "We are credibly informed, that the ministerial troops in Boston are dying fast with the scurvy; that it is judged their stores cannot hold them many weeks." [6]

Accounts of atrocities, designed to stir Americans to hatred of the

British troops, also found space in the *Mercury*. One of the first reports from Concord, published on May 1, told that the British, on their arrival in the Boston suburb, had searched the house where John Hancock and Samuel Adams had lodged during meetings of the Massachusetts provincial congress. Not finding the two men, "the inhuman Soldiery Killed the Woman of the House and all the Children, and set Fire to the House."

Gaine was kept busy printing the war news, but he also took advantage of the patriotic fervor to promote other goods he sold at the Bible and Crown. He printed and sold a copy of the latest military exercises. And to the shelves of books, stationery, and medicines, he added two new items: "DRUMS and FIFES, American Manufacture." [7]

Despite his Whig leanings at this point, Gaine was unable to allay completely the suspicions of Whig readers who remembered his Tory sympathies in the days following repeal of the Townshend Acts. Whigs still monitored the *Mercury* and other newspapers for the slightest hint of pro-British tendencies. In the issue of March 11, 1776, Gaine printed a traveler's report that Parliament had given approval to a restraining bill under which "all American Property, whereever found, after the 5th of January 1776, will be confiscated"; that twenty officials had left England "with unlimited Powers, to make Peace with the Americans"; that 50,000 Russian and Hessian troops were scheduled to sail for the colonies in the spring; and that Colonel Guy Johnson, Ethan Allen, and about thirty other Americans were being held prisoner in England. On receiving complaints that the item "gave Offence," Gaine explained in the newspaper that he had published only what the traveler, a Mr. Temple, had told a number of people in the city. "And the Person who informed me of the same (a well-known Friend to the American Cause) is willing to be qualified on the Subject, if the Public should require it." [8] This explanation, apparently, was published for the benefit of the Sons of Liberty who, while more restrained, were still powerful.

The radicals, as always, were quick to vent their displeasure at printers who ran counter to them. Gaine was well aware of the fate of "Jemmy" Rivington. That Tory editor printed in his *Gazetteer* of March 2, 1775, that the New York committee of observation had deferred nomination of delegates to the second Continental Congress. The story hinted at dissension among the members. Branding the report "entirely and wholly false and groundless," the committee appointed Philip Livingston and John Jay to question Rivington. When Livingston and Jay reported back that Rivington had told them he had printed the account out of "common report," the committee resolved "that common report is not sufficient authority for any Printer in this City to publish any *matters as facts* relative to this Committee, and tending to expose them to the resentment of their Constituents, and the odium of the Colonies." [9]

Rivington's outspoken disdain for the Whigs brought damning resolutions from committees of observation and inspection throughout the colonies. He was accused of being "impelled by the love of sordid pelf, and a haughty and domineering spirit," and his *Gazetteer* was described as "being filled with pieces replete with falsehoods and mere chicanery, only designed, as we believe, to divide and lead astray the friends of our happy Constitution." [10] Rivington was forced into hiding by threats of physical harm before the provincial congress intervened with a recommendation that he not be molested "in his person or property." [11] The Sons of Liberty ignored the congress, however, when they learned that Rivington was planning to print a pamphlet by the Pennsylvania Tory Joseph Galloway, *A Candid Examination of the Mutual Claims of Great-Britain and the Colonies: With a Plan of Accommodation on Constitutional Principles.* [12] On November 25, 1775, a party of seventy-five horsemen led by Isaac Sears, an official of the Sons of Liberty, drew rein at Rivington's front door. Gaine may have watched from his print shop down the street that noontime as the men destroyed Rivington's press and rode off to Connecticut with his type. Rivington fled to England. Undoubtedly, Gaine was determined not to be forced into exile; however, one wonders what

Gaine's reaction would have been had he known that Rivington carried with him a secret appointment as royal printer, retroactive to January 1, and would be back within two years to claim that position.

The Rivington incident must have convinced Gaine—if he was not already convinced—that the Sons of Liberty would not tolerate dissent. But if he needed further assurance, he could look at the case of Samuel Loudon, an immigrant from Scotland who had set up in business as a ship chandler, then a bookseller, before establishing the *New-York Packet* in January 1776.[13] Loudon at once made the newspaper a Whig organ; however, he made the mistake of agreeing to print an answer to Thomas Paine's revolutionary pamphlet *Common Sense*. When he announced plans for its publication, a group of radicals broke into Loudon's home, forced the printer from bed, and destroyed the manuscript of the reply and what type had already been set.[14]

Certainly Gaine must have received a copy of the broadside warning printers of the city that if they were to "print or suffer to be printed in your press anything against the rights and liberties of America, or in favour of our inveterate foes, the King, Ministry, and Parliament of Great Britain, death and destruction, ruin and perdition shall be your portion."[15] Gaine might well have felt, as Loudon did, that the "freedom of the Press is now insulted and infringed. . . . A few more nocturnal assaults upon printers may totally destroy it, and *America,* in consequence, may fall a sacrifice to a more fatal despotism than that with which we are threatened."[16] But if he did feel that way, Gaine remained silent, and continued to tread a cautious path.

Americans reached the critical juncture in their relations with the mother country in 1776. Already at war, they would have to find a basis for compromise with the crown or declare independence. Compromise seemed impossible; independence was too momentous a step. Great debates on the question filled the hall at Philadelphia where the second Continental Congress was meeting, and these were mirrored in the newspapers.

The newspaper debate was precipitated by the publication in

January 1776 of Paine's *Common Sense,* "the most influential piece of Whig propaganda since the 'Farmer's Letters,'"[17] and a frank call for independence from Great Britain. But the verbal battle was not waged between Whigs and Tories. According to historian Arthur M. Schlesinger, the Tories were no longer a potent force in the formation of American public opinion; rather, the Whigs themselves split into three camps, the disunionists, like Paine, the reunionists, and "the fence sitters, who had not yet made up their minds."[18] All opposed Great Britain, but they disagreed on the methods of opposition.

Gaine strove for neutrality in the debate; possibly he hoped that showing the clash of ideas would help his readers determine the right course to follow. Opening the *Mercury*'s columns impartially to the most influential essayists in the disunion and reunion camps, he printed the writings of "Cato," "Cassandra," and "The Forester." None of these appeared in the *Mercury* first; Gaine reprinted their utterances from James Humphreys's Tory *Pennsylvania Ledger* and the Whig *Pennsylvania Gazette* of William Sellers and William and David Hall.

"Cato," the Reverend Doctor William Smith, provost of the College of Philadelphia, was the first to appear in the *Mercury.* In a series of eight letters published between March 18 and May 6, he argued that independence was unjustified. On March 25 he urged that representatives of the Continental Congress meet with the British commissioners sent to negotiate a peace and stated: "I am bold to declare, and hope yet to make it evident to every honest man, that the true interest of America lies in *reconciliation* with Great Britain upon *Constitutional principles,* and I can truly say, I wish it upon no other terms." In a subsequent essay, published on April 1, he did not rule out the possibility that the colonies would have to break with the mother country, but "if we should now affect *Independency* as our own act, before it appears clearly to the world to have been forced upon us by the cruel hand of the Parent state,—We could neither hope for *Union* nor *Success* in the attempt."

"Cassandra"—James Cannon, a mathematics tutor at the same

college—was a militant disunionist. He had provoked Smith's attack by an essay in the *Pennsylvania Evening Post* in which he had argued that the peace commissioners should be arrested on their arrival in America. Faced with the rebuttal by "Cato," he reiterated his position that the British ministry could be trusted on only one point. He wrote in the April 1 *Mercury* that they would "divide and conquer the Americans in any way they could." "Cato," however, countered Cannon by saying: "He seems to have drank [*sic*] deep of the *cup of independence;* to be inimical to whatever carries the appearance of *peace;* and too ready to sacrifice the happiness of a great continent to his favourite plan." [19]

One writer, "A Common Man," urged both sides to avoid such *ad hominem* arguments as "Cato" and "Cassandra" resorted to and to discuss only the issues.[20] Gaine recognized that Thomas Paine did just that and he reprinted three essays that Paine had signed "The Forester." Paine sided with "Cassandra" and directed his polemics at "Cato." His argument was eloquent in tone but simple to understand: there could be no such thing as reconciliation because of the British ministry's past treatment of America.[21]

Gaine might have been expected to side with the Catos of the colonies; instead, he seemed to favor independence. He filled the *Mercury* with petitions from throughout the colonies declaring support for the Congress should it vote to sever the ties with Great Britain. From only a few areas came expressions of opposition.[22]

The Cassandras saw their dreams made reality with the Declaration of Independence. When it was proclaimed on July 4, 1776, Gaine was elated. "Yesterday the CONGRESS unanimously Resolved to declare the *United Colonies* FREE and INDEPENDENT STATES," he reported in the *Mercury* of July 8, 1776. When the Declaration arrived in New York, Gaine published it on the front page of the July 15 issue of the newspaper. On the inside pages he reported that when the document was read to the troops of the Continental Army it was "everywhere received with the utmost Demonstrations of Joy." For the benefit of his subscribers living outside New York, Gaine reported that a joyous crowd toppled the statue of George

III, which had stood near the fort since the repeal of the Stamp Act, and carefully preserved the lead for bullets; they then released the debtors from jail. Gaine and his workmen had no time for these celebrations; they were kept at work printing the Declaration as a broadside to be distributed throughout the town.[23]

Independence brought more than rejoicing; it also brought hardships. After the cheers had died away and the fireworks had cooled, the colonists were faced by the evils that the Tories had predicted. Within a month after the Congress had assumed for Americans the "Separate and equal Station to which the Laws of Nature and of Nature's God entitle them," [24] it was reported in the New York provincial convention that provisions in the city were "very scarce and dear." [25] Nonimportation had squeezed off the flow of goods from England, and prices of hard-to-get domestic items spiraled.

Printers found newsprint most difficult to obtain. Neither type nor ink was readily available. Journeymen were called to the tasks of war. Unlike many printers, Gaine did not reduce the size of the *Mercury*. But his advertisements for linen rags appeared more frequently, and on July 29 he was forced to make another humbling appeal to his readers to pay their bills:

The great Expence, and uncommon Difficulty and Trouble that attends the Printing-Business at present, and in particular that of publishing a Newspaper, at this Juncture, must be well known to the Readers of this Paper; 'tis therefore hoped our Customers will, as soon as possible, think of discharging their Accounts, that the Printer may be the better enabled to carry on his Business and serve the Public to their Satisfaction.

Difficulties were not only economic. Through the summer a fleet of British warships lay at anchor off Sandy Hook, and Gaine reported in the *Mercury* of August 19 that American troops from neighboring colonies were marching toward New York to reinforce its defenders. Gaine reported a widespread fear: "Every tide we expect an Attack will be made on this City from the piratical Fleet at Staten-Island." Fear was so great that General Washington

urged the state convention to order the removal of women, children, and the infirm of the city.

Any doubts that Washington's fears were real were erased in
late August. On the night of August 22–23, a group of patriots
led by John Lamb took possession of the British artillery on the
Battery, just to the east of Fort George. A British barge close to
the shoreline spotted the activity and in the exchange of gunfire
which followed one of the sailors aboard the barge was killed. The
news spread to the barge's mother ship, the *Asia,* commanded by
Captain George Vandeput; Vandeput ordered his gun crews to
fire on the Americans and quick pulls on nine lanyards sent a
salvo of eighteen- and twenty-four-pound shot crashing into the
city.[26]

Gaine did not report the event in the next issue of the *Mercury,*
that of August 26; perhaps he believed it superfluous to publish
news everyone knew already. But in his next issue he had even
more frightening news: on August 28 the British landed fifteen
thousand men on Long Island; within hours the redcoats had
routed Washington's raw American troops, who fled from the
battlefield in disarray and began to retreat to upper New York
state. Gaine, however, reported on September 2 that the colonials
"fought and fell like Romans." In the same issue, he sneered at
the loss of the British General Grant, while exaggerating for
propaganda purposes the size of the general's army: "Thus fell the
Hero, who boasted in the British House of Commons, he would
march thro' America with 5000 Men, having only Marched five
Miles on Long Island with an Army of more than four Times the
Number."

Despite his tone of bravado, Gaine, like his fellow New Yorkers,
undoubtedly was seriously demoralized by the American defeat.
Even worse, the British now threatened Manhattan Island. As
Freneau had Gaine describe the aftermath of the battle:

But when they [the British] advanced with their numerous fleet,
And Washington made his nocturnal retreat,

> (And which they permitted, I say, to their shame,
> Or else your New Empire had been but a name)
> We townsmen, like women, of Britons in dread,
> Mistrusted their meaning, and foolishly fled; . . .

Even the able-bodied were packing furniture and other household goods onto carts and wagons and fleeing the city. The narrow streets were jammed with shouting men and their frightened families. Iron-rimmed cart wheels clattered on the stone pavements. Here and there a forgotten and yelping dog scurried about looking for his departed master.

The printers fled with the rest of the population. John Anderson, who had begun his *Constitutional Gazette* in August 1775, closed the newspaper after just one year of publication. John Holt went to New Haven; his *Journal* would lie dormant for nearly a year, when the New York Provincial Congress would call on him to revive the newspaper at Esopus, later Kingston, New York. Loudon, who had decided by the middle of August to leave and had successfully sought appointment as state printer, advertised that he was "removing his Printing-Office to Fish-Kills, where the Provincial Congress now reside." [27] But even with the support of the Congress, Loudon would not be able to resume publication of the *Packet* until January 1777.

Whether Gaine had sent his family out of the city earlier is not known, but in the second week of September, according to Freneau:

> Like the rest of the dunces I mounted my steed,
> And galloped away with incredible speed,
> To Newark I hastened, . . .

After the battle of Long Island, Gaine stayed in New York only long enough to oversee preparations for the *Mercury* of September 9, but he had left for Newark by the time the newspaper was issued.[28] He left no record of the trip, but perhaps he took the same route as did a refugee British Army officer who, later in the month, left New York in early morning and crossed the Hudson to Powle's

Hook. Then by taking the stage overland, as the officer did, Gaine
could have arrived in Newark in time for dinner in the evening.

With him, the printer took one press and a limited supply of
paper and type for the newspaper and a quantity of Bibles, writing
paper, quill pens, "Maredant's Drops," and "Keyser's Famous Pills
. . . for curing all disorders incident to Soldiers in a Campaign"
for the shelves of his new shop.[29] Oddly enough, he left the Bible
and Crown open and in the care of a shopman, but it is not known
whether he made plans to return to New York before he left. Re-
gardless, his sojourn in New Jersey would be brief and he would
return to the city which the British now occupied.

CHAPTER 11

Patriot in Newark

Gaine, industrious as always, was the first of New York's refugee printers to resume publishing his newspaper, and at fifty he became a pioneer in New Jersey printing history. His was only the fourth newspaper to be published there, and after he left, no other newspaper followed until 1791, when John Woods's *Newark Gazette* appeared.

The first issue of Gaine's transplanted newspaper came from the press on September 21. Only one sheet, printed on both sides, it was still designated the *New-York Gazette; and the Weekly Mercury,* probably because of the difficulty of having a new nameplate cast, but it bore the legend "Printed at Newark in East-Jersey." Its news, gathered "since our last printed in New-York the 9th Instant," consisted primarily of foreign news gleaned from London newspapers which the printer undoubtedly carried with him on his flight from New York. Domestic news was comprised almost entirely of information about American troop movements, including an account of the American withdrawal from New York and the British occupation of the city. Gaine also reported that in the early morning of the day the newspaper was issued, September 21, "a dreadful fire was discovered from the heights back of this town [Newark], which upon the appearance of daylight was sup-

posed to be the city of New York in flames." Subsequent issues
of the Newark *Mercury,* issued on Saturdays rather than Mondays
as the New York newspaper had been, differed little in content.

On September 30, nine days after Gaine's Newark newspaper
appeared, the printer must have been surprised to see another *New-
York Gazette; and the Weekly Mercury* appear. More puzzling
still, and certainly aggravating, particularly because he had since
published another Newark edition, the nameplate of the newspaper
stated that it was "printed by Hugh Gaine." The second *Mercury,*
however, was the responsibility of the British authorities in New
York. As soon as they had occupied the town, the British moved
to establish a newspaper to replace those the American printers
had withdrawn. On September 25, Governor William Tryon asked
the newly-arrived Ambrose Serle, private secretary to the British
admiral Lord Howe, and the Reverend Charles Inglis "to under-
take the management of the political Part in the News Paper about
to be published." [1] Both accepted, with Serle becoming the senior
partner in the enterprise.

Serle was thirty-three years old. Four years earlier, when William
Legge, the second earl of Dartmouth, became secretary of state for
the colonies, he appointed Serle an undersecretary. Later, the young
undersecretary served as solicitor and clerk of reports for the Board
of Trade. An English Tory with middle-class values, Serle had long
been convinced that the colonial revolution was criminal. In 1774
he had dealt with the question in a paper, "Sketch of an Essay on
Adjusting our Disputes with the Colonies," a defense of the united
empire; a year later, he published *Americans against Liberty: or
An Essay on the Nature and Principles of True Freedom, Shewing
that the Designs and Conduct of the Americans Tend Only to
Tyranny and Slavery.* In the latter, he concluded that "the Rebel-
Americans, in the wildest Delusion and by the worst of Means, are
avowing themselves THE OPEN ENEMIES TO THE PUBLIC AND
GENERAL LIBERTY OF THE BRITISH EMPIRE." [2] His writings in
the *Mercury* were to reflect the same bias.

Shortly after his arrival in New York with the occupation force,

Serle had gone to the Bible and Crown to buy newspapers. He found that although Gaine had fled, the printing office was open and in the care of a shopman, possibly James Penny, who worked for Gaine between 1776 and 1778. Serle also discovered that the printer had left behind a press, type, and other printing materials. Since these were available, Serle and Tryon decided to revive the *Mercury* rather than start an entirely new newspaper. The day after his meeting with the governor, Serle returned to the print shop and began preparations for publishing.[3]

It was apparently an oversight that put Gaine's name on the first issue of the British-run *Mercury;* his name did not appear again. Certainly, the florid writing style was not Gaine's, as readers could determine from an apology addressed to them in the September 30 issue:

The Printer trusts the Candor of his readers will excuse the late Want of Intelligence from England, when they consider how entirely the Channel of Communication has been stopt by the present Commotions. He hopes, however, to have it in his Power in future, to furnish the Public with the earliest Accounts from Europe, and with the most punctual Information respecting the present Transactions in America.

Serle filled much of his editorial space with announcements by the occupation authorities, but that was not a completely new departure for the newspaper; Gaine, in his role as public printer, had frequently published extracts from the votes and proceedings of the assembly and the proclamations of the colonial governors and the mayors of New York. Neither did the two men differ in the small amount of space which they gave to New York news; both clipped freely from newspapers from abroad and from the other colonies. They did differ in the proportionate amounts of space they gave to foreign and domestic news. We have seen that as the revolutionary movement gained momentum Gaine devoted greater space to accounts of colonial events. Serle reversed the trend and gave the greater part of his editorial columns to reports from abroad, particularly from Britain, as the patriot propagandist Thomas Paine would note later in one of his *Crisis* essays.

This is not to say that Serle was not a conscientious news-gatherer; he was, and he took pride that "nothing . . . is inserted [in the news columns] as New York Intelligence, but Matters of Fact as they have arisen." [4] He sometimes strayed from his standard, however, and on at least one occasion Lord George Germain, secretary of state for the colonies, worried that falsehoods in the newspaper would "bring discredit upon the rest of the intelligence." [5] Serle also made a travesty of objectivity by coloring his news with a vigorous pro-British tone. On October 21, 1776, for example, in an account of an American foray onto Staten Island, he reported:

A body of the Rebels skulked over from the New-Jersey Shore to Staten-Island, and, after cowardly setting Fire to two or three Farm-Houses, skulked back again to their former Station. Probably, from their Conduct, it may be judged that these were the People who, about the middle of last August, committed such an Act of villainous Barbarity, as cannot be recited without indignation. A very little Boy, belonging to an Officer of the Army, was playing by himself upon the shore of Staten-Island, opposite the Jerseys, when about seven or eight of the Rifle Men or *Ragged Men,* came down slyly, and discharged their Musquets upon him. Immediately upon the poor Creature's falling, they gave three cheers and retired. This was a most cruel, dastardly, and infamous murder upon a defenceless, innocent Child. Such Poltroons will always run away at the Appearance and Approach of Men!

Gaine's account in his New Jersey newspaper of October 19 contrasted sharply:

Last Wednesday morning a party of our people, consisting of about 1200 men, under the command of Colonel Griffen, went from Amboy to Staten Island; and at the same time a party of about 500 set off from Elizabeth Town Point: The command from Amboy soon fell in with a number of the King's troops, killed two, and brought off 18 prisoners, among them 8 Hessians. We had two men killed, and Colonel Griffen wounded in the foot.

Another point of difference between Gaine and Serle was the view the two men held of the editor's role. Gaine, of course, was first and foremost a printer and, as already noted, he believed that he should not present himself as a writer in his own newspaper or "appear in print in any other Manner, than what merely pertains to . . . [his] Station of Life." When he was attacked by the Presbyterian faction in the controversy over the establishment of King's College in 1753, he had defended himself in the *Mercury* only after repeated insults and then "only with the greatest Reluctance." [6] In contrast, Serle was not a printer but a writer; and, in that respect, he came closer to fitting the definition of a modern editor than did Gaine.

Under new direction, the New York *Mercury* did not slight the news. But, since Serle did not supervise the printing operations but left that to a shop foreman, he could devote his time and efforts to the writing of essays. His first piece appeared in the issue of October 28, 1776, under the pseudonym "Irenicus." Americans were guilty of "timidity of conduct" on the battlefield, he wrote, and this was due to the "badness of their cause, and the doubtful opinion which in general they entertain of it." Loyalist Americans, however, were cut from different cloth: "The conduct of those Provincials, who acted with the King's Troops upon Long Island, may serve to prove, on the hand, that Americans can act worthy of their descent, under the influence of loyal principles, and in the company of Britons."

A second "Irenicus" essay followed on November 18, 1776; and on December 30 of the same year, another of Serle's essays appeared over the signature "Publicola." Beginning in February 1777, he published a series of eight essays which he signed "Integer." [7] In the first of these, according to his own account, he "endeavored, with some Drollery, to shew the Expence, that Must arise to America, under the Establishment of a Govt. by the Congress." [8] He proposed himself, as "Integer," for the "Office of *Accomptant General* [*sic*] to the HIGH AND MIGHTY UNITED STATES OF NORTH AMERICA," to handle the finances of what he considered to be an incompetent Continental Congress:

Their imagination cannot descend to such mean Business, as the stating and reckoning of Sums; and, therefore, they suppose that either calling for Money at Random, or calling a Substance by the name of Money, which for the Soul of me, I believe to be nothing better than a common Piece of Paper, will fully answer every Purpose of War and Peace, and settle all Things upon their favourite Foundation.

"Integer" totaled the sums he expected would be expended on the civil and military establishments, which he estimated at £6,000,000 or "probably . . . four Times the Sum; and especially if we feel bold." He concluded:

Our old Mother-country would have supported and protected us at one TWENTIETH *Part of the Expence; which it will cost us to defend and secure ourselves; and when we have done all that we can do, we shall not be one* HUNDREDTH *Part so* SECURE *nor a* THOUSANDTH *Part so* HAPPY, *as we were before.*[9]

The British and the American Loyalists were duly appreciative of Serle's biting humor; the essayist "had the Satisfaction to hear, that . . . ['Integer'] was well received by the best People upon the Spot, and that they believed the Irony, as well as the Matter, wd. have a good Effect." But while his writing brought him compliments, Serle gained even greater satisfaction from his essays because they allowed him an outlet for his sense of patriotism. He confided to his diary: "If the Interests of my dear Country be served, and this flagitious Rebellion be broken, I shall rejoice in any and every Means taken to accomplish it." [10] He grew confident that his means would have his intended effect, for he was convinced of the "almost incredible Influence these fugitive publications [newspapers] have upon the People." [11]

Gaine, in the meantime, was besieged in New Jersey by economic difficulties and doubt. Freneau would have him say: "trouble and care/Got up on the crupper and followed me there!" The poet's observation, if anything, was an understatement. Gaine may have chosen Newark as a refuge because his son had attended Mr. Had-

don's school there; he undoubtedly had accompanied the boy to
Newark after vacations and was familiar with the town. Possibly,
too, he had friends there. But familiar surroundings and friend-
ships would mean little if he could not support himself and his
family, particularly the children. The oldest child, Elizabeth, was
only fifteen in 1776; John was fourteen; and Anne, barely twelve.
Of the two youngest, Cornelia was probably not yet six, and little
Sarah was just four. The children must have shoes and dresses,
hot porridge and beef, and with his meager income, Gaine was
hard put to provide them with those necessities. In Newark he
could no longer be concerned with amassing wealth; life now became a matter of survival.

As already stated, Gaine had carried only a limited amount of
type with him in his escape from New York and it was nearly
impossible to replace; lead that might have been used in founding
letters was being melted and cast into bullets instead. Paper, too,
was scarce. Obviously, he could no longer depend on the output of
his Long Island mill; importation of paper from England was impossible, and wartime conditions prevented a sufficient and reliable
supply from Pennsylvania. It must have been with great reluctance
that, on September 28, he reduced the size of the *Mercury* by half.

His account books, as he confessed to Richard Varick, aide to
General Philip Schuyler, were "in such a situation, as puts it out
of my power to render you an exact state of General Schuyler's
account with me since June 1775, but as near as I can think, 'tis
about £45. Should it be more or less it can be easily rectified." [12]
Schuyler at least wanted to pay his bill; others of the *Mercury's*
normal readership had been scattered by the war, and those who
did take the newspaper rarely could afford to pay for it. On October 12, Gaine entered a telling plea to his subscribers:

This paper has now been published in this town four weeks, and
sent to the customers, that could be found, as usual. The great and
uncommon expence attending the carrying on business at this juncture,
obliges the publisher to request those in arrears to discharge their
accounts, which will be gratefully acknowledged.

Even if he was paid, payment would likely come in the nearly worthless Continental currency which Serle, as "Integer," had lampooned.

At the same time, Gaine must have compared the lack of advertising on his pages to the revenue-producing display in the New York newspaper. For the first issue of the Newark *Mercury*, the full-size single sheet, he had been able to put together slightly less than a full column of advertising and one of the notices, the largest on the page, was one of the printer's own. Gaine's second issue, a folio half the size of its New York counterpart, was made up of twelve columns, but only two columns of advertisements— the equivalent of less than a full column in Serle's *Mercury*, since the Newark newspaper's columns were also narrower. In each of Gaine's final four issues in Newark, he had advertising enough to fill only three of his diminutive columns. In contrast, the first issue of Serle's newspaper, that of September 30, contained only one full column of notices. But the usurper, as Gaine must have considered him, built his advertising volume steadily to three columns, then to five columns.

With only a cursory glance at the New York newspaper's advertising, Gaine must have realized that business, dormant in Newark, was getting back to normal in New York. The notices placed in the Newark *Mercury* were composed almost entirely of offers of rewards for deserters from the army, runaway slaves, or lost livestock; less than a quarter of them advertised goods for sale. No wonder that in his *Gaine's Universal Register, or American and British Kalendar, for the Year 1777*, the printer dismissed Newark and the whole state of New Jersey by saying, "In this Province there are no Towns of any Importance." [13]

By reading the New York advertisements, Gaine obtained quite a different picture. He could almost visualize distiller Richard Deane stocking and restocking his shelves of wine and rum for his red-uniformed customers; Moore and Neale presiding over their grocery sales; Valentine Nutting, one of Gaine's newest competitors for the book and stationery trade, counting his day's receipts; and,

at his own Bible and Crown, an unfamiliar face methodically reading newspapers or giving orders to print as a pamphlet "A Sermon
Preached at St. Paul's, New York, September 22, 1776." [14] It could
not have been a pleasant daydream; and, added to it, were other
fears.

The printer heard, too, the rumors that the British were planning
to attack New Jersey. He was aware of weaknesses in Washington's army and undoubtedly noticed, as did a British officer who
made his way through the thinly-picketed American lines, that
while the Continental troops were numerous, they were also
"ragged, dirty, sickly, and ill-disciplined." [15] From Gaine's point of
view, according to Freneau:

> . . . your army I saw without stockings or shoes,
> Or victuals—or money, to pay them their dues,
> (Excepting your wretched Congressional paper,
> That stunk in my nose like the smoke of a taper,
> A car load of which for a dram might be spent all,
> That damnable bubble the old Continental,
> That took people in at this wonderful crisis,
> With its mottoes and emblems, and cunning devices;
> Which, bad as it was, you were forced to admire,
> And which was, in fact, the pillar of fire,
> To which you directed your wandering noses,
> Like the Jews in the desert conducted by Moses)
> When I saw them attended with famine and fear,
> Distress in their front, and Howe in their rear;
> When I saw them for debt incessantly dunned,
> Not a shilling to pay them laid up in your fund;
> Your ploughs at a stand, and your ships run ashore.

Because of the army's situation, Gaine had to consider not only
how he could continue to feed and clothe Cornelia and the children, but what he could do for them if the British did invade.
Where would they go if the redcoats came? Philadelphia? No,
that was bound to be a major military objective. The wilderness?
They had known nothing but the comforts of town life. Could

they keep running indefinitely? And how could he provide for them, since he knew only the printing trade? What if the British subdued the Americans in the end, as seemed likely at that point? What then? These questions, whispered to Cornelia in the night so as not to disturb the children, suggested only one answer—return to the relative safety of New York.

The printer also may have shared with Cornelia the gossip of the print shop and the disturbing tales he had heard of confusion and discord even in the ranks of the revolutionary leaders. One could even question who those leaders were. Were they duly constituted officials like his old adversary from the triumvirate William Livingston, who was now governor of New Jersey? Or were they the chairmen of the vigilantelike committees of inspection, who suspiciously examined the *Mercury* for the least hint of Tory sympathies? Or the untrained Army officers who seemed incapable of leading even their own men?

Gaine spoke of the news he had heard from Philadelphia, that some of the congressional delegates had deserted to the British. Among his fellow refugees, in fact, "some of the most Intelligent People," seeing the progress of the British and the plight of the Americans, had begun to "think more justly of the Cause of [the British] Government" [16] and had returned to New York. Gradually, Gaine came to believe that "the People in general would embrace Reconciliation but for the inflammatory Declamations and Instigations of their Preachers," [17] the predominantly Whig Presbyterians with whom Gaine, as a faithful Anglican, had clashed for so many years. In all, it seemed foolish to endure the sacrifices required in the face of almost certain disaster.

In the last week of October, Gaine gave instructions for the printing of the *Mercury* of November 2, the seventh issue published at Newark, but he did not stay to see his orders carried out. In Freneau's words:

> . . . after remaining one cold winter season
> And stuffing my papers with something like treason,

And meeting misfortunes and endless disasters,
And forced to submit to a hundred new masters,
I thought it more prudent to hold to the one—
And (after repenting of what I had done,
And cursing my folly and idle pursuits)
Returned to the city, and hung up my boots.

On the morning of November 1, while Washington's rag-tag army was retreating from the British on the battlefield at White Plains, Gaine gathered his family and returned to New York. So hurriedly did he leave Newark that he left press and eleven boxes of type behind; ironically, these were later confiscated by the New York Provincial Congress and lent to John Holt to help him revive his pro-American *New-York Journal*.

Gaine's odyssey to loyalism was over; he would stand solidly in the Tory ranks for the remainder of the war. His stance would bring him the hatred of the Whigs; but, ironically, because of his sojourn with the Americans, he would not be fully trusted by the British.

CHAPTER 12

With the Redcoats

꒰꒱ Returning to New York, Gaine and his family probably re-
traced the route of their exile, traveling overland from Newark to
Powle's Hook, where they boarded a ferry (perhaps bribing the
ferryman) and slipped through the American and British lines
back to the city. In Freneau's description, Gaine did not make the
trip without trepidation:

> Ashamed of my conduct, I sneaked into town,
> (Six hours and a quarter the sun had been down)
> It was, I remember, a cold frosty night,
> And the stars in the firmament glittered as bright
> As if (to assume a poetical stile)
> Old Vulcan had give them a rub with his file.

The New York that the family returned to on November 1 was
a different city from the one they had left in September. Immediately before the American withdrawal it was "empty and desolate;
you would scarce see any person or but a few in the streets." [1] The
defending soldiers, then, wore uniforms of brown homespun or,
if they were fortunate, the blue of the Continental Army. A back-
drop of British canvas billowed in the harbor. Now, as the sun

rose that brittle November morning, Gaine saw the city under British occupation; it was a scene which changed little throughout the war.

The naked masts of firmly anchored British men-of-war rose from the harbor to the southeast and in front of them lay a skeleton city of charred and broken walls and chimneys left by the fire of September 21. The wind on the morning of the fire had been strong and had blown the flames the length of Broadway, from Whitehall at the south, near Fort George, up to St. Paul's Church. Somehow, St. Paul's had been spared, but Trinity Church, Gaine noticed with sadness, was totally destroyed. In the Trinity ashes were many of the records of his own family—the birth certificates of his children and the paper attesting to his marriage to Sarah Robbins.

Gone, too, were many of the homes of those of his friends who lived on the west side of town. Of those houses which had been spared by the fire, some had already been occupied by the British; others would soon be appropriated for their use. Among the houses they took for their own, number 3 Broadway was the office of the secretary to General William Howe, the army's commander-in-chief; at number 24 Broadway was the Royal Artillery hospital. Turning east on Wall Street, Gaine noted that number 7 was occupied by General Lossberg and number 10 by Colonel Morse, the army's chief engineer. At number 10 in Gaine's own Hanover Square lived Admiral Robert Digby. Gaine's family were allowed to retain their house, but they were required to quarter Ensign Campbell in the "lower Room" beginning in 1779.[2]

A kaleidoscopically uniformed soldiery paraded in the streets. With the English, in their redcoats and "glittering and gallant pomp," had come a colorful variety of allies, and Gaine had difficulty identifying them for his wide-eyed and questioning children: Hessians with towering, brass-fronted caps, flowing moustaches blackened and glistening with boot dye, their hair plastered down with tallow and flour; Scot Highlanders with checkered tams, red coats, tartans flung over their shoulders, and kilts which left their "knees exposed to the view and the winds"; Grenadiers of Anspach, with towering black caps; and gaudy Waldeckers in cocked hats edged with yellow.

After debarking, the Gaines made their way through the soldiers and the smoke-blackened streets to Hanover Square, on the east side of town. Fortunately, the winds of September 21 had pushed the fire away from the Square, sparing the two- and three-story houses which lined Queen Street. The Bible and Crown had survived, and the printer found little physical change there. The bustle of the print shop was familiar; Gaine saw his compositors setting type and the apprentices dampening paper in preparation for printing the *Mercury* of November 4. Serle stood by, perhaps editing one of his own essays while supervising the workmen.

Gaine may have eyed Serle suspiciously and, as the printer introduced himself and the two sat down to discuss the war, he probably found Serle not entirely to his liking. Serle showed his disdain for the Americans in general and for printers, whom he found "more tardy" in America than in London,[3] in particular. After all, he was secretary to Lord Howe and he was accustomed to the company of such upper-class Americans as the Reverend Doctor Inglis and Governor Tryon. Faced with this rather haughty, self-satisfied Englishman, this usurper, Gaine may have squirmed, his temper well-provoked. But he was in a humble—and humbling —position, as Freneau showed in "Hugh Gaine's Life":

> 'Till this cursed night, I can honestly say,
> I ne'er before dreaded the dawn of the day;
> Not a wolf or a fox that is caught in a trap
> E'er was so ashamed of his nightly mishap—
> I couldn't help thinking what ills might befall me,
> What rebels and rascals the British would call me,
> And how I might suffer in credit and purse,
> If not in my person, which still had been worse: . . .

Quietly, Gaine spoke of his disillusion and the doubts of the other refugees in New Jersey. He passed on intelligence of American military strength and told Serle that Benjamin Franklin had sailed for Europe the week before to try to secure the aid of the French court for the Americans. Serle noted the information for his diary and, undoubtedly, for his British superiors.[4]

Apparently, Gaine did not immediately begin work; the first issue of the *Mercury* after his return did not bear his name. Ironically, the November 14 newspaper carried an account of a battle at Lake Champlain "taken from a Paper printed at Newark, in East New-Jersey." Serle may have inserted the item to twit Gaine, for the latter had printed in his last newspaper at Newark the New York news of October 7 from "the *New-York Mercury,* printed in New-York, at the house lately kept by Mr. Gaine." [5]

The following week, while Serle spent most of his time in his quarters, Gaine took over day-to-day operations. In the issue of November 11, his name returned to the nameplate; within, he printed his familiar advertisement announcing that Keyser's Pills could be obtained at the Bible and Crown.

Gaine was not his own master, however. Serle continued to exercise over-all supervision, and he was ultimately responsible for everything which Gaine pulled from his press, including the infamous *Military Collections and Remarks,* a book Gaine published in 1777. The author, Major Robert Donkin of the British army, evidently contracted with Serle to print the book before Serle left New York because the dedication was dated March 1, 1777; perhaps it had even been published by that time. *Military Collections and Remarks* was intended to be a serious study of the art of war and, as such, it might have gone unnoticed by the Americans; but it contained a series of footnotes which made the book, its author, and its publisher, hated. In his introductory remarks, Donkin related his general principles to the particular situation in America; and, commenting on the first battles of the Revolution, he noted that "there was one [British] soldier scalped and his ears cut off (though not quite dead) at Concord-bridge by these barbarians: two captains, who saw him wallowing in blood will prove this, should any rebel dare deny it." [6] In discussing the treatment of prisoners of war, Donkin appended the following note:

The savage, barbarous and most torturing cruelties (far exceeding those exercised by Papists upon protestants in England, Ireland and France) of the american rebels to the king of England's liege subjects, totally excludes these miscreants from any christian appellation whatever! I will only mention one instance among many, which is more infernal than tarring and feathering? viz. stripping a man naked, putting him cross legs on a rail full of splinters (cleft triangularly) the sharpest edge upwards, then carrying him on shoulders 'till he expires (for they won't let him fall off) huzzaing, a tory, a tory! *Monstrum! horrendum! informe! Dei cui lumen ademptum!* [How evil! how dreadful! how hideous! God, light of life!] [7]

These accusations angered the Americans; but another note, on the use of bows and arrows, roused them to fury:

Dip arrows in matter of small pox, and twang them at the American rebels in order to inoculate them; This would sooner disband these stubborn, ignorant enthusiastic savages, than any other compulsive measures. Such is their dread and fear of that disorder! [8]

The Americans were quick to twang venomous epithets at Gaine for publishing such writings. The *Pennsylvania Journal*, in a "New Catechism," asked: "Who is the greatest liar upon earth?" The answer: "Hugh Gaine, of New York, printer." [9] A mock—and mocking advertisement later appeared in the same newspaper:

Wanted for his Majesty's service, as an assistant to his Excellency General Howe and Hugh Gaine, printers and publishers of the New York Gazette, a gentleman who can lie with ingenuity, Enquire of Peter Numskull, collector and composer of lies for their Excellencies at New York. N.B.—A good hand will receive the honor of knighthood. [10]

John Dunlap devoted nearly all of the February 18, 1777, issue of his *Pennsylvania Packet, or the General Advertiser* to a parody of the *Mercury* entitled "The IMPARTIAL CHRONICLE, or the INFALLIBLE INTELLIGENCER; upon the plan, after the manner of, the NEW-YORK MERCURY." Included in the issue was an advertisement similar to those Gaine often printed to announce his publications:

Printed by Hugh Gaine, and given gratis, The Mirror of Mercy, or the Primrose of Favour and Conveniency; shewing that every total American may preserve the free possession of his whole estate, real and personal, by suffering the British Parliament to deprive him of nine-tenths of it; edited by his most gracious Majesty's most gracious plenipotentiaries. Certainly nothing can more fully demonstrate the infatuation of the rebels, and their woful [sic] seduction by a few artful and ambitious demogogues.

A second notice purported to be the publisher's statement of ownership:

Printed and sold by Hugh Lucre, under the inspection and by permission of martial authority, in New York, in Gasconading Square, opposite to Rhodem— —ntado Alley, at the sign of the Crown against the Bible, where all persons may be supplied with False Intelligence for hard money, and with Truth upon no terms whatsoever.

Thomas Paine, in the second of his *Crisis* essays, also lashed out at the printer. Referring sarcastically to the overwhelming amount of news from Britain which filled the *Mercury,* he wrote: "We can tell by Hugh Gaine's New York paper what the complexion of the London *Gazette* is." [11]

But it was Serle, in his supervisory capacity, who deserved the opprobrium of the revolutionaries. It was he who reveled in the fact that "the Rebel News papers, as well as the Author of the *Crisis,* shew great Spleen at the New York Gazette, which gives me some Proof that it has good Effect, and that my Labor & Superintendence of it have not been thrown away." [12] When he sailed for Philadelphia in July 1777 with Lord Howe's fleet, he severed his connection with the newspaper, content "with the Satisfaction . . . of doing some Service to the Cause of my King and my Country." [13] But it can be questioned whether he would have enjoyed being the direct target of invective had he not had Gaine for a foil. Gaine, judging from his reactions to other attacks which had been made upon him, certainly must have been angered by the slurs; but he was in no position to defend himself against them.

With Serle's departure, Gaine once again took charge of the newspaper completely, but he soon found his privileged relationship with the authorities changed. James Rivington returned to New York in September 1777, and the British, shunting Gaine aside, confirmed Rivington's appointment as royal printer at £100 per year. Perhaps unaware of the appointment, Gaine greeted Rivington's arrival almost ecstatically in the *Mercury* of September 29:

This Gentleman, with unparalleled Fortitude, having nobly disdain'd to usher to the World any inflammatory Pieces, which might be productive of introducing Anarchy, instead of Constitutional Authority, into this once happy Country, felt, in the severest Degree, the Rage of popular Delusion.—*Liberty* he always firmly adher'd to; Licentiousness from his Soul he ever detested.

But Gaine was less enamored of the laced-cuff dandy when, after the taking of Forts Montgomery and Clinton by the British in the fall of 1777, he was forbidden to publish the news until Rivington had printed it. He confided to his diary: "This Day by Order of the Commandant [General Valentine] Jones, I was ordered to desist from printing an Account of the taking of the . . . Forts, and shortly after in the same Day, Mr. Rivington issued the Account as Printer to his Majesty." [14] Gaine was both hurt and angry; but he realized that his outspokenness in favor of the revolution in the Newark newspaper had left him suspect in the eyes of the British. But, jealous as he was at Rivington's success, Gaine announced to the public on October 8: "A *particular* Account of the Operations . . . in the Attack and taking the Forts . . . will be published this Day, from *good Authority,* by JAMES RIVINGTON, PRINTER TO THE KING'S MOST EXCELLENT MAJESTY." At least one benefit accrued to Gaine as a result of Rivington's appointment, however, even if neither man realized it at the moment—

the revolutionaries immediately turned the greater part of their invective against Tory newspapers on the royal printer.

Rivington was not entirely satisfied with the name of his newspaper as simply *Rivington's New-York Gazette*. On October 18, 1777, he changed it to *Rivington's New-York Loyal Gazette,* but that did not properly signify his official position and on December 31 of that same year he began entitling it the *Royal Gazette.* But whatever "Jemmy" called it, to the American patriots it was known only as "Rivington's Lying Gazette." [15]

John Holt and Samuel Loudon, printing for the Americans in upper New York state, had problems not unlike those of Gaine and Rivington. In August 1775 Holt and Loudon had left New York, Holt going to New Haven, Loudon to Fishkill. Loudon had received appointment as official state printer with a yearly allowance of £200 on condition that he revive his *New-York Packet,* which he did in January 1777. Almost immediately, however, he fell into disfavor among certain members of the Provincial Congress for printing extracts from Gaine's *Mercury.*

According to Loudon, he had clipped the excerpts and had begun printing them when an official got wind of the matter and told him not to publish them. Mindful of the repercussions that had followed his attempt to print a rebuttal to Paine's *Common Sense* two years earlier, Loudon set about remaking the page. Unfortunately, however, he had left some sheets drying in the print shop, and a few were taken away by visitors, others by the Albany post rider. Loudon feared reprisals by the Committee of Safety; but, as he told them later, he feared even more the "mischief" that would ensue if he tried to get the sheets back and his attempted suppression were made known.

When word got around that the sheets had been distributed, the Committee was indeed interested; it demanded to know why and how. Loudon explained that he had originally decided to publish the excerpts "with no evil design but merely to satisfy the curiousity of those who might wish to see what stuff was published at New York."

After deliberating privately, the Committee severely reprimanded him. "Mr. Loudon," Chairman James Livingston said, "I am directed to inform you that by publishing your paper after an express order of this house to the contrary, you have been guilty of a great insult to their authority, that so long as you receive a pension from this house you are their servant and therefore guilty of great ingratitude in presuming to disobey their commands. The house do not mean today any restrictions upon the liberties of the press, but they are determined not to employ any person who shall do things inimical to the cause of American freedom." But, Livingston also told him, "the House upon your submission have pardoned this offence." [16]

Not all members pardoned him. Soon after, machinery was put in motion to replace Loudon with John Holt. Only nine days after Loudon's appearance, the Committee of Safety, on a motion by John Jay, appointed a three-man committee to persuade Holt to set up a printing office in Esopus. The three, John Broome, Henry Wisner, and Henry Schenck, were authorized to offer Holt £200 a year, the same fee given Loudon, if he would print a public newspaper "on like terms as Samuel Loudon." As a further inducement, the Committee made available to Holt the eleven boxes of type Gaine had left behind at Newark. Holt accepted, and in the summer of 1777, renewed publication of the *New-York Journal.*[17]

Two new pro-British newspapers made their appearance in the city of New York during the Revolution. James Robertson, who, with his brother Alexander—"two Scots Paper Spoilers," Parker had called them[18]—had published the *New-York Chronicle* in 1769 and 1770, returned to the city and, in January 1777 established the *Royal American Gazette.* In September 1779 William Lewis entered the competition with his *New-York Mercury; or General Advertiser.*[19] With the publication of the latter, New Yorkers were given the benefit of a newspaper every day except Sunday, for in May 1778 Rivington made the *Royal Gazette* a semiweekly, published on Wednesday and Saturday, and five months later, Robertson began semiweekly publication of the *Royal Ameri-*

can Gazette, on Tuesday and Thursday. Gaine's *Mercury,* of course, was still published on Monday, while Lewis's *Mercury* came off the press on Friday.[20]

To oversee these newspapers, the British appointed a licenser, whom they paid 20s. per day. But it was an office which Serle, at least, on a visit to New York in April 1778, found "useless . . . & an addl. Expence!" [21] Censored or not, the newspapers provided news aplenty for all, and newspaper vendors roamed the streets hawking their wares "with yells in every pitch of the human voice, from the 'childish treble' to the bassoon sounds of a tall fellow, who roared in tones of thunder, 'Bloody news—bloody news— bloody news—where are the rebels now?' " [22]

Each of the Tory publishers colored his pages in accordance with the wishes of the British authorities, and even though he had been slighted, Gaine was no exception. His reversion to the British side was complete. In private conversations he swore "vengeance against the Jerseys," [23] apparently for the failure of the government there to support him, and in the *Mercury* he attempted to carry out his oath with tactics not unlike those he had employed earlier in the American cause.

Gaine had few scruples about the methods he used to promote the British cause. The *Mercury* of March 9, 1778 carried forgeries of what were said to be resolves by the Continental Congress declaring that American troops who left the service on the pretext that their enlistments had ended would be caught and treated as deserters. The forgeries caused consternation among the American military command. It was difficult enough to secure enlistments and maintain morale; and George Washington damned the forgeries as "infamous to the last degree, and calculated to produce the most baneful consequences." [24]

The Tory printer also played down, when he did not ignore, British weaknesses and defeats; at the same time, he spotlighted those of the Americans. In the fall of 1777, for example, the Americans under General Horatio Gates defeated General Burgoyne's forces at the battle of Saratoga—a victory of immense importance in convincing the French to lend their aid to the revolutionaries. As usual, there was only sketchy news from the battlefield, and Gaine worried about Burgoyne's fate. Then came news that Burgoyne's "whole army [was] taken by Capitulation."[25] Gaine entered the report in his diary but he did not carry the news in the *Mercury* of the following day, nor even in the next issue, on November 3. In the latter, he reported only:

As no Accounts, properly authenticated, of the Situation of the Northern Army, have yet been brought to this City, the Printer entreats the Public to excuse his inserting any of the Reports that have been circulated, until he may be warranted by Intelligence derived immediately from General Burgoyne.

In the issue of November 10, more than a month after the battle, Gaine at last informed his readers of the truth, that the Americans had triumphed. But he did not say so directly; rather, he published only the articles of surrender, which he had taken from a Boston newspaper of October 6.

Similarly, Gaine withheld for more than a month the news that Sir James Wallace, a British naval commander, had been captured by the French fleet. Although he was aware of Wallace's capture as early as October 16, 1779, he did not print the news in the *Mercury* until November 22, and then it was subordinated to dispatches telling that the British had repulsed a major French threat to Georgia.

With the most momentous news of the war, Lord Cornwallis's defeat at Yorktown, Gaine was more prompt. He ignored the news in the first issue of October 22, 1781, but the following week, October 29, he printed General Washington's letter to the Continental Congress reporting that "a reduction of the British army under the command of Lord Cornwallis, is most happily effected."

Gaine's general policy was one which he had tacitly criticized in his Newark *Mercury* of November 2, 1776, by reprinting from a London newspaper an editorial reaction to biased news from the battlefield. Condemning "the finesse and cunning evasions of the

Scottish Gazette, which exceeds that of Brussels in impudence and falsehood," the writer continued:

> If an engagement happens at sea, we hear nothing of the ships which are taken from us. If any are taken from the enemy, though the bulk of an oyster boat, we are sure to have it added to the list in the Gazette. . . . If Howe is forced from Boston with ten thousand men, who were to have conquered all America, the Gazette calls it 'a resolution to remove;' if he leaves only two hundred pieces of cannon, and one half of the King's stores, it says, he leaves nothing behind him.

In practicing such eighteenth-century news management, Gaine showed that he realized the effect of news presentation on both civilian and military morale. Accounts of British successes would bolster the hopes of the redcoats and the Tory population; ignoring their failures would keep them in blissful ignorance and would do nothing to improve American morale.

Gaine also knew that newspaper accounts could be valuable sources of military intelligence for the enemy. The British read the newspapers of the revolutionaries for such information; Gaine occasionally brought to Serle's attention newspaper items which might have intelligence value.[26] The Americans sought such information from the Tory press; and the *Mercury* on at least one occasion, had given them information about British fleet movements.[27] But Gaine and Serle generally were cautious about providing news which might help the Americans, much to the annoyance of some of the American leaders. As Alexander McDougall, the American Wilkes who now wore the stars of a general, wrote to Washington:

> You may rest assured, from undoubted authority, that the utmost pains are taken in New-York to keep *European* intelligence from the fleet and army; for two packets past, the boats from them are not suffered to land, or any of the crew even to go on board the Admiral. . . . Although a packet arrived there the 15th Instant, yet *Gaine* has not inserted one paragraph of European Intelligence in his paper since,

but the address of the Corporation of York to the King, and General *Howe's* being made a Knight of the Bath.[28]

Gaine contributed to the British war effort in other ways as well. As we have noted, he quartered a British ensign named Campbell in the "lower Room" of his home, even though his large family was cramped for space. The printer gave up an apprentice, Benjamin Crofts, in the summer of 1780, when the British navy called for volunteers to serve with the fleet. And, at the age of fifty-six, Gaine became a member of the Mayor's Battalion, a volunteer city militia. The organization built fortifications around Manhattan Island in 1782 and patrolled the town when the regulars were away.[29]

Freneau lampooned Gaine's hospitality to the ensign and the printer's service with the militia:

> You, doubtless, will think I am dealing in fable
> When I tell you I guard an officer's stable —
> With usage like this my feelings are stung;
> Six hours in the day is duty too hard,
> And Rivington sneers whene'er I mount guard,
> And laughs till his sides are ready to split
> With his jests, and his satires, and sayings of wit:
> Because he's excused, on account of his post
> He cannot go by without making his boast,
> As if I was all that is servile and mean . . .

But, while Gaine may have found these duties onerous, he performed them uncomplainingly. And all of his efforts for the British were not so rigorous.

More to the printer's liking, he was one of a group of "loyal adherents of the crown and the episcopal church" who kept the New York stage alive during the British occupation.[30] He and the other members of the group transformed the John Street Theatre into the Theatre Royal in which the "characters were performed by gentlemen of the [British] Army and Navy." [31] Gaine collected the rent and sold the tickets.

Gaine did not neglect his own business during the war years. He kept the Bible and Crown stocked with stationery and other writing supplies, "Navy Journal Books ready rulled [*sic*]," "Dram Bottles, covered with Leather," *"Elegant* Pocket Pistols," and a wide variety of other items. Medicines on his shelves included "Ryan's Worm-destroying Sugar Plumbs," "Dr. James's Fever Powder," "Bateman's Golden Spirit of Scurvy Grass," and, as ever, Keyser's Pills, "So well known all over *Europe,* for their superior Efficacy and peculiar Mildness, in perfectly eradicating every Degree of a certain DISEASE, without the least Trouble or Confinement." [32]

From his press came not only Donkin's *Military Collections and Remarks,* but a number of other military publications, including *The Manual Exercise, as ordered by his Majesty in 1764* and *Rules and Articles for the better Government Of His Majesty's Horse and Foot Guards, And all other His Forces,* both issued in 1777. He printed his usual variety of almanacs and sermons; and he also published, among others, George Fisher's *The American Instructor,* (1777), James Hervey's *Meditations and Contemplations* in two volumes (1778), *Grammatical Institutes; Or, An Easy Introduction to Dr. Lowth's English Grammar,* by John Ash (1779), and the medical text, *Cases of the Angina Trachealis, With the Mode of Cure,* by Richard Bayley (1781).

Such books, published with increasing frequency during the war years, were soon to become the staples of his shop. For with the peace, Gaine realized that the *Mercury* would be no more welcome among the Americans than the continued presence of British troops; and when the redcoats withdrew in the fall of 1783, Gaine retired his press from politics. On November 10, a little more than thirty-one years after the appearance of the first issue of the *Mercury,* Gaine published the final issue of the newspaper. The other Tory publishers also recognized the futility of trying to continue under the Americans. All but the cocky "Jemmy" Rivington. In the absurd belief that his newspaper would be tolerated, Rivington dropped all references to being "Loyal" or "Royal" and, on November 22, 1783, assumed for it the nonpolitical title *Rivington's New-York Gazette, and Universal Advertiser;* the *Universal Advertiser* appeared for only a month, however.[33]

The last major item of news to appear in the *Mercury* was George Washington's farewell to the American Army. Gaine described the general as "the worthy and most esteemed American Fabius" and, in so doing, he gave some credence to the generally accepted conclusion, expressed by Freneau, that he would

> . . . always adhere to the sword that is longest,
> And stick to the party that's like to be strongest: . . .

and that his press

> . . . that has called you (as tyranny drove her)
> Rogues, rebels, and rascals, a thousand times over,
> Shall be at your service by day and by night,
> To publish whate'er you think proper to write; . . .

But without his newspaper, Gaine would no longer give support to any faction. Instead, he would settle quietly into the life of post-Revolution New York and, ultimately, would lose the stigma of loyalism.

CHAPTER **13**

A Printer of Good Reputation

꿈 The immediate postwar period saw the flight from the new United States of thousands of Loyalists; it has been estimated that some thirty-five thousand may have left New York alone. Many more, however, remained, and Gaine joined these in an effort to make a new life under a new government. But there is no evidence that he ever petitioned the state government for asylum, as Freneau suggested in "Hugh Gaine's Life":

> To the Senate of York, with all due submission,
> Of honest HUGH GAINE the humble Petition;
>
> . . . .
>
> THAT, since it is plain we are going away,
> You will suffer Hugh Gaine unmolested to stay.

Rather, with the withdrawal of the British forces from the city he merely discontinued the *Mercury*, brought down the crown from his shop sign, removed it from his colophon, and quietly went on with his printing and bookselling business "at the Sign of the Bible" in Hanover Square.

The printer perhaps regretted that his loyalism forced him to withdraw from the newspaper business. The influence of the press had soared during the war and Americans had become habitual and avid readers of newspapers; this was apparent, particularly in

New York. Loudon returned with his *Packet,* and Holt offered the *Independent Gazette; or the New-York Journal Revived.* New on the scene, appearing within two years after the peace, were the *New York Evening Post,* a triweekly; the *New York Gazetteer,* a daily; the weekly *Independent Journal;* and the *Daily Advertiser.*[1]

But if Gaine had regrets, he did not waste time brooding. He kept himself and his press busy turning out broadsides, pamphlets, and books. Almanacs were still a yearly feature of the press, as they were with most early American printers. In addition, Gaine published a variety of children's books, including *The History of Little Goody Two-Shoes* and *The Mother's Gift: or, a Present for All Little Children Who Are Good,* both printed in 1785; guides to conduct, such as John H. Moore's *The Young Gentleman and Lady's Monitor, and English Teacher's Assistant* and *The Young Clerk's Vade Mecum: or, Compleat Law Tutor,* which Gaine printed in 1787; and reprints of such popular English works as *An Essay on Man* by Alexander Pope (1786), Richard Brinsley Sheridan's *The School for Scandal* (1786), and the second part of *The Rights of Man* by Thomas Paine (1792). The shelves of the "Bible" bulged with these works and a large inventory of imports from Britain, Scotland, and Ireland. In a catalogue of the latter, issued in 1792, Gaine listed more than five hundred titles.

The new leadership of the country did not withhold printing contracts from the former Loyalist. In 1784 he printed the *Laws, Statutes, Ordinances and Constitutions, Ordained and Established by the Mayor, Aldermen, and Commonality of the City of New York;* in 1788 he received a contract to print money for the state; the following year, the two-volume *Laws of the State of New York* came from his press; and in 1790, he printed *United States Regulations for the Order and Discipline of the Troops of the United States,* written for the army by the military hero Baron Friedrich Wilhelm von Steuben.

The success of his printing and bookselling business following the war testifies to Gaine's reinstatement in the community. Few, apparently, harbored resentment against the printer for his aid to the British. That this should have been so is understandable; more British sympathizers lived in New York during the war than in any other colony, and most of them stayed when the British troops departed. The Whigs who returned to the city when hostilities ended were in the minority; the former Tories lived and worked among the majority. Still, Gaine seemed to make his way easily among his one-time enemies. His neighbors repeated the story that shortly after the end of the war the printer met the poet Philip Freneau on the street. Gaine, though smarting from the verbal lashing Freneau had given him in "Hugh Gaine's Life," was more than friendly.

"You are a clever fellow," Gaine remarked. "Let me have the pleasure of taking you by the hand. Will you walk around the corner and join me in our parlor? We will take a glass of wine together. You, sir, have given me and my paper a wide reputation." [2]

Whether Freneau accepted, as Ethan Allen was said to have accepted a similar invitation from Rivington, is not known, but a fellow New Yorker testified that their political hostility did not carry over into their personal lives. Freneau, Gaine, and even Rivington became "all in harmony, notwithstanding the withering satire against those accommodating old tories by the great bard of the revolutionary crisis." [3]

Not all were willing to forget the old animosities completely, however. When the New York legislature chose Gaine to print the state's money in 1788, Loudon complained to Governor George Clinton that they did not choose "a whig printer." [4] Loudon and his son had been Whigs, the *Packet*'s publisher stated, and while he had "no doubt but Mr. Gaine can print the money well—we can do it as well." Yet, the next year, when the city of New York staged a grand parade to celebrate the adoption of the Federal Constitution, Gaine and Loudon, "those veterans of the type and quill," rode together on a float at the head of "the printers, book-binders, and stationers." The two old printers supervised a miniature shop in which "the press was plied briskly, and impressions of a patriotic ode distributed, as they were taken [from the press], among the multitude. Their banners were worthy of their proud vocation." [5]

Gaine was not merely a showpiece in that parade; he was a celebrant, for he had been one of the signers of a "memorial of sundry citizens" of the city which requested of the legislature "that measures be taken for receiving that District into the American confederacy as a free and Independent State." He had come to think of himself as a citizen of the new nation, even to the point of recording in his diary the "great Mirth and Festivity" attending the Fourth of July and the celebration of George Washington's birthday.[6] As the United States experienced the pitfalls of finding its place in the world community, Gaine could "tremble when I think of the Situation of America." [7]

As might have been expected, Gaine was a Federalist when political parties emerged from the Hamiltonian and Jeffersonian conflicts of the Washington Administration. He believed with the Federalists that the threat posed by a rapacious France required that America link its fortunes to British military power, as it wisely did. For that reason he followed closely the mutinies in the British navy in the 1790s; he predicted that "should the British Fleet be destroyed, the French will be the Masters of Europe." Were that to come to pass, he noted ominously in his diary: "Take Care America." [8] Similarly, he was suspicious of the American negotiations with the French Directory which became known as the XYZ Affair. He confided to his diary: "It would not surprise me to hear that the French long ago had seized all the American Property in their Kingdom, and perhaps commit all Americans to Goal [sic]." [9]

Gaine's preference for the British and his mistrust of the French once again placed him with the minority. As one observer, John W. Francis, noted, "Jealousy of Britain, affection for France, was now the prevailing impulse." [10] When a French frigate arrived in New York harbor, the townspeople marched with the crew from dockside to the home of the French consul. According to Francis, who shared the crowd's pro-French sympathies, the parade paused before the shops of Gaine and Rivington, who both

were snugly ensconced behind their shop counter[s]; Rivington in
rich purple velvet coat, full wig and cane and ample frills, dealing out
good stationery to his customers; and Gaine, in less ostentatious cos-
tume, ready with religious zeal to dispose of his recent edition of the
Book of Common Prayer to all true worshippers.[11]

It may have been on that same occasion that a barber named
Huggins visited French sailors aboard their frigate in the harbor
and, on leaving, gave them his card and asked that they honor him
with their business. Subsequently, some of the sailors came on shore
and began asking where they could find Huggins. As they pronounced the barber's name "Hoo-ganes," however, they were soon
directed to the sign of the Bible in Hanover Square. The Fran-
cophobe printer was not amused and testily sent the Frenchmen on
their way, all the while muttering uncomplimentary references to
Huggins.[12]

Although Gaine took no active role in politics, he took part in
civic affairs. He was a vice-president of the New York Hospital
and a principal in the movement to revive the New York Society
Library, the city's first loan library. When the library was established in 1754, he had become a charter member along with such
men as Mayor Whitehead Hicks, William Livingston, John Morin
Scott, and his old partner in the paper mill, Henry Remsen. He
maintained his membership by paying annual dues of ten shillings;
and when the library was reestablished in 1788, he was elected a
trustee. He served with such distinguished fellow citizens as
Chancellor Robert Livingston, Robert Watts, Daniel Crommelin
Verplanck, and Remsen, all of whom were later described as
"gentlemen of education and culture"; and, in April 1793, he was
reelected to another five-year term. In 1789, Gaine had published
the first edition of *The Charter, Bye-Laws and Names of the
Members of the New-York Society Library*.

Gaine was instrumental in forming a trade association for
booksellers. In 1802, along with Matthew Carey of Philadelphia,
he helped to found the American Booksellers Association, which

grew out of the American Literary Fair held in New York earlier that year. The New York printer became the organization's first president, and under his leadership it conducted a system of annual book fairs which were the forerunners of modern-day trade sales.

Gaine's later years allowed him freedom to indulge his long-standing interest in the theater. As we have seen, he had printed and sold theater tickets as early as 1761 and had helped to keep the New York stage alive during the war years. The *Mercury* from time to time had carried reviews of plays, even though Gaine "was not a discriminating critic—he was simply an approving friend, and, like the commendations of many modern writers on the stage, his praises were apt to be warmest when they were least deserved." [13]

Gaine was an intimate of theatrical manager William Dunlap and Dunlap's actor associates, Lewis Hallam and John Hodgkinson. He acted as a witness in a partnership agreement the three men made, loaned them money, and at one point acted as an intermediary when Hallam and Hodgkinson had a falling-out over Mrs. Hallam's role in the company. She was an actress of doubtful talent and with a fondness for drink which made her performances somewhat unpredictable. Early in 1797, Hodgkinson, a sensitive actor, refused to allow Mrs. Hallam to appear with him. She reacted by stalking onto the stage while Hodgkinson was performing and denouncing him in front of the audience. The actor, enraged, withdrew from the agreement with Hallam and Dunlap and wrote a pamphlet, published by J. Oram, one of Gaine's competitors, giving his side of the controversy. [14] Hallam then served notice that he would not act in any of the company's plays unless his wife also was allowed to play.

As manager, it was Dunlap's problem to reconcile the dispute so that the playhouse, which had closed, could be reopened and so that the three men could be saved from financial destruction. He appealed to Gaine, a friend of all the parties involved. The printer agreed with Dunlap that "Hallam could only be saved from ruin by withdrawing his wife from the stage, and undertook to deliver a letter to him stating that her continuance in the theatre would prevent the fulfilling of the recent engagement." [15] But Gaine reported back to Dunlap that Hallam was adamant and advised Dunlap privately that Mrs. Hallam "would be your destruction." As negotiations dragged on, Gaine pressed Dunlap for concessions. It might be better, the printer told him, to accede to Hallam's wishes and let the woman "convince the public of her worthlessness." [16] Partly through Gaine's efforts, and partly through concessions by Hodgkinson and Dunlap, Mrs. Hallam did return to the stage and the dispute ended.

At about the same time, a group of 130 men invested in a new theater which was to be built in Park Row. Gaine served on the committee representing the group and negotiated a four-year lease with Dunlap and Hodgkinson. The venture was a trying financial burden, especially in the building stage. With the structure still unfinished in the spring of 1798, the committee reported that they had spent the original subscription of $42,375 and had incurred an additional debt of $85,000. Even when complete, the building was not entirely satisfactory. As Dunlap described it later:

The waste, mistakes, and mismanagement in erecting this building are perhaps unexampled. The useless excavations under the stage and pit remain as testimonies, for though the house has been rebuilt and burnt, and rebuilt again, these yawning abysses still remain, and, though covered over, will long remain monuments of "alacrity at sinking." [17]

There is no evidence, however, that Gaine suffered financially.

The printer was assured of a comfortable life because of his earlier investments in real estate. He owned twelve lots near the tip of Manhattan Island. Four of the lots, twenty-five by eighty feet each, lay on the west side of Greenwich Street. He now lived with his wife and his spinster daughter, Anne, at 179 Greenwich, two blocks west of Broadway. Four other lots, also twenty-five by eighty, lay on the east side of Washington Street, and the remaining four—double lots—lay just to the west, running through from Washington Street to West Street. [18]

In the spring of 1794, Gaine leased from Trinity Church ten

lots of what was then called the Church Farm. Each was twenty-five feet wide and one hundred feet long and extended from the southwest corner of Greenwich and Desbrosses Streets to the Hudson River or to what is now the eastern edge of the West Side Highway. As part of the conditions of the lease, which he secured for forty-two years, Gaine was to level and pave the streets bounding the lots, and thus he became one of the earliest developers of the town as it extended north from its early Wall Street boundary. The following year, Gaine leased for twenty-one years three additional lots from the church, each of them twenty feet front and rear and seventy-five feet on each side. These were located at the southwest corner of Greenwich and Reade Streets.

In addition, Gaine owned a plot of sixty-five acres in the country about four and one-half miles northeast of the city hall on part of old Lispenard holdings. He no longer traveled about on foot, but rode out to the grounds in befitting style in a horse and carriage, and in 1802 he built a manor house on the estate. The printer described it as having a "kitchen, with cellars, a handsome room suitable for a housekeeper or nursery, and 4 rooms for servants" on the first floor. On the second were two large rooms on either side of the hallway with "convenient parlors between them." Another hallway ran the length of the third floor and two large rooms stood on either side, "with dressing rooms between them, and a garret over the whole house." On the grounds he grew asparagus and a variety of fruit trees.[19]

Gaine lived in the house only a short time when early in 1807, shortly before his death, he advertised it for sale. Why he sold it is uncertain, but perhaps a key lies in the advertisement itself: "The house is double and well calculated to accommodate a large family." Gaine no longer had a large family. His son was dead, and three of his four daughters were married.

Gaine's daughters had made advantageous marriages after the war. Two of them married brothers and, in so doing, joined a family that contained old political enemies and allies of their father. Cornelia married Anthony Rutgers, a merchant-trader based

in Curacoa, in the lesser Antilles, on April 17, 1790, in a ceremony
which featured one of the bridegroom's schooners tied up at an
East River dock. The ship was "decorated in honor of the occasion
with a very numerous variety of the colors of all nations and exhibited a most beautiful appearance." [20] Five years later, on
November 21, 1795, Sarah married Anthony's brother Harmon,
who owned an auction house at 145 Pearl Street, across from
Gaine's "Bible."

The Rutgers brothers, descendents of a Dutch brewer who
emigrated to New York in 1636, were part of the family which
aided substantially in the establishment of Queen's College in New
Jersey, and for whom the college was later renamed. An ancestor
had been a juror in the Zenger trial of 1735. Their first cousin,
Helena, was the wife of John Morin Scott, one of the triumvirate
which had so stirred Gaine's ire in the 1752 and 1764 religious
controversies, and another cousin was Samuel Provoost, rector of
Trinity Church and, later, the first bishop of the Espicopal Church
consecrated in America. Thus, if they had not been already, the
old religious battles were resolved by marriage. Elizabeth Gaine
was married on May 21, 1803, to John Kemp, a distinguished
professor of mathematics, natural philosophy, and geography at
Columbia College.

Elizabeth had no children; but Cornelia and Sarah together
presented their father with five grandchildren. Cornelia and
Anthony had two daughters and one son: Cornelia Matilda, born
on February 17, 1791; Anthony Gaine, born four years later; and
Mary Gouvernor, born on May 27, 1799. Sarah and Harmon had
two sons and they honored the old printer by naming their first
born after him. The second was christened Harmon, for his father.

Gaine had established his son John as a printer and bookseller
in Pearl Street, near his own shop, in 1785. Perhaps he had dreams
of a father-son partnership, but John died two years later at the
age of twenty-five, and Gaine took as a partner Phillip Ten Eyck.
Gaine and Ten Eyck operated the bookstore until 1807, but they
gave up printing about 1800, selling the business to Alexander

Ming and William Young, who proudly advertised themselves as "successors to Hugh Gaine."[21] Ming and Young were among the pioneers in the field of business newspapers, publishing the *New-York Price Current,* one of the earliest financial newspapers in America. Ming on his own later established another business newspaper, the *Daily Item.*

Hugh Gaine died on April 25, 1807. The *Columbian Centinel,* which had erroneously carried his obituary on May 8, 1805, printed another. The *New-York Evening Post* also noted his passing.[22] Neither mentioned the old animosities; the religious and political battles had long since been forgotten, and his British sympathies during the war were forgiven. To the paragraphers he was simply Hugh Gaine, printer.

To historians of the history of American journalism he became "the turncoat,"[23] or the "turncoat patriot editor."[24] One characterized him as "double-dealing";[25] still another wrote: "When with the Whigs, Hugh Gaine was a Whig; when with the Royalists, he was loyal; when the contest was doubtful, equally doubtful were the politics of Hugh Gaine."[26] But, as we have seen, the printer's political course is not so easily explained.

His path to loyalism was, indeed, an odyssey. During the thirty-one years in which he published the *New-York Mercury,* Gaine pursued a course dictated by ambition and expediency. He vacillated between first one faction, then another; between principle and principle; and between rewarding hand and rewarding hand. The evidence suggests that he was essentially an apolitical man, devoted primarily to economic survival; patriotism was only a secondary consideration. Like other Americans of the time, particularly those of the merchant class, Gaine fit the description offered by social historian Vernon Parrington: "So long as his customary and traditional rights remained undisturbed, the colonial would throw up his cap for King George; but if he were driven to choose between loyalty and self-interest, between sentiment and profit, the choice was certain."[27]

Consider Gaine's opposition to the Stamp Act. The act increased the price of paper and Gaine was dependent upon that commodity for the conduct of his business. He fought the measure because of the heavy financial burden of the duties. In the Townshend Acts crisis, Gaine was willing to protest what he felt were oppressive acts of the British ministry, particularly because of the duty on paper, and he supported, at least in the *Mercury*, the nonimportation movement. But, along with the majority of other colonial merchants, he wished to limit opposition within clearly defined bounds; when the British retreated, that was the time for the colonists to fall back also.

His essentially conservative attitude was reinforced by the violent excesses of the Sons of Liberty. Gaine feared not only British reprisals, especially after Parliament's vindictive measures against Massachusetts, but also the ire of the Sons of Liberty, which, if completely unleashed, would destroy all that he had built. At the same time, he could not side completely with the British, even after the first Continental Congress, in assuming legislative authority, "raised the ultimate question of allegiance." [28]

Three explanations for his course are possible. First, Gaine did not wish to alienate either Whig or Tory lest he jeopardize his investment in the *Mercury*. This is the easiest explanation to accept in view of his devotion to self-interest. But, on the other hand, each side already had devoted journalistic servants. Gaine may well have believed that it was his duty to publish a newspaper which was essentially neutral.

The third and most plausible explanation encompasses aspects of both of the others: Gaine chose neutrality because he did not wish to anger either of the two political camps and because he did not want to pit the *Mercury* against the direct economic competition offered by the Whig Holt or the Tory Rivington.

Why did Gaine, then, wholeheartedly espouse the American cause after Lexington and Concord? He could not have done otherwise. By the time war came, the conservatives had lost control of the protest movement; the Sons of Liberty brooked no pub-

lished dissent, as was evident in the cases of Loudon and Rivington. Had he published an antipatriot newspaper he would not have
published it long. Thus, again, it was his economic self-interest
which dictated his course.

That he fled New York on the eve of the British occupation of
New York is not surprising in view of his year-long support of the
Americans. He believed that the Americans would shelter and
support him if he continued to aid them, whereas he faced possible
punishment at the hands of the British for publishing against
them.

Self-interest, too, was at the heart of his decision to defect to the
British. His difficulties in publishing in New Jersey in the turmoil
of war were compounded by the fact that the British had
stabilized life in New York and, more important to him, had taken
over his printing shop and had revived the *Mercury*. In addition, a
patriot's testimony that he heard Gaine swear "vengeance against
the Jerseys" indicates that the printer may have met with some
abuse at the hands of the Americans there because of his former
Tory associations. Furthermore, the British overseer of the
Mercury, Ambrose Serle, was an editor, not a printer; Gaine was a
printer first and then an editor. The British may well have bribed
Gaine to return to complement Serle's talents. However, there is
no evidence to support this assertion except Gaine's own history of
serving the man who held out the greatest reward.

A host of remote factors probably also entered into his decision.
Leonard Labaree, a student of the American Loyalists, has listed
five groups of persons who were most likely to have embraced
loyalism: officeholders; Anglican clergymen and their parishoners
in the North; Quakers and other conscientious pacifists; large
landholders, especially in the North; and merchants.[29] Gaine can
be located among each of these groups, with the exception of the
Quakers.

Gaine had served the provincial government and its conservative leadership for nearly a decade as public printer, and like his
fellow officials he had taken an oath of allegiance which, to many

—and perhaps to him—was "more than empty words." He was an Anglican, and he may well have been among those for whom "the mere fact of membership in the Anglican Church" was a strong influence impelling toward loyalism. Certainly, as a faithful churchman, he could not have been immune to the efforts of his ministers to "preach submission to the State and make the Church a bond of union and an effective force for the maintenance of royal authority." [30] At the same time, while Gaine's landholdings could not be described as large in comparison with the holdings of such families as the Livingstons and Lispenards, they were substantial; and possibly he feared that if he were to remain with the Americans and the British were to win the war, as seemed likely at the time, he would lose his real estate. Lastly, his printing and bookselling business and his proprietorship of the paper mill had made him a wealthy merchant and he stood to lose all for which he had worked for so long if the British triumphed.

All of these factors forged a compatibility with the British; and, because he was apolitical, in his own mind, he was deserting only physical surroundings, not an ideology. In contrast to the men who made the Revolution, Gaine had no strong political beliefs for which he was willing to risk his life or his fortune. Instead, he sacrificed what historians have seen as his honor in allying himself with the crown. But, as Henry Bamford Parkes observed:

History is not kind to lost causes, and if [the Americans had lost the war] . . . the fathers of the American republic would presumably have been remembered as a discredited group of radical adventurers, while Loyalist leaders like Hutchinson of Massachusetts, De Lancey of New York, and Galloway of Pennsylvania would have figured as the real heroes of the conflict. [31]

So, too, might Hugh Gaine have been remembered, not as a turncoat, but as one of only a handful of heroic newspapermen who risked the hatred of their neighbors and the condemnation of history to support a glorious—because victorious—cause.

Deserter though he had been, Gaine nevertheless had made a

contribution to American journalism and to the American nation. In publishing his newspaper for thirty years he had helped to lay the basis for the journalism that would come later and had helped to instill in Americans the habit of newspaper reading. Perhaps more important, the *Mercury* devoted itself to American issues in the period prior to the Revolution; and in so doing, the newspaper helped to forge a national identity which both foreshadowed and contributed to the making of a separate American nation.

Gaine was buried in the family vault on the south side of Trinity Churchyard; his son John had been buried in the vault twenty years earlier, and four years after her husband's death, Cornelia was interred with them. The stone that marks their grave is reddish-brown in color, weathered with age, and lies flat and level with the ground. No historical society or hereditary organization has erected a monument to Gaine, such as the ones which mark the nearby graves of Alexander Hamilton, William Lewis, a signer of the Declaration of Independence, and the pioneer printer William Bradford; the stone contains no explanation of his course in life nor any pleas for the passerby to remember who lies there. Only his name identifies the person buried there and only rarely does a visitor pass who knows, as did Freneau,

> That he once was a printer of good reputation,
> And dwelt in the street called Hanover Square,
> (You'll know where it is, if you ever was there)
> Next door to the drug-shop of doctor Brownjohn,
> (Who now to the dog-house of Pluto is gone)
> But what do I say—who e'er came to town,
> And knew not HUGH GAINE at the Bible and Crown.

NOTES
BIBLIOGRAPHY
INDEX

Notes

1 Apprentice to Publisher

1. H. R. Plomer, G. H. Bushnell, E. R. McC. Dix, *A Dictionary of the Printers and Booksellers Who Were at Work in England, Scotland and Ireland from 1726 to 1775* (Oxford: Oxford University Press, 1932), p. 394.

2. Ibid., p. 408.

3. "Hugh Gaine's Life" appeared in *The Freeman's Journal; or, The North-American Intelligencer* of Philadelphia in installments in the issues of January 8, January 29, and February 12, 1783. Freneau based the poem on an alleged petition to the New York state legislature in which Gaine asked permission to remain in the state after the cessation of hostilities. However, there is no evidence that the printer submitted such a petition. The poem, in slightly revised form, appears in Fred Lewis Pattee, ed., *The Poems of Philip Freneau, Poet of the American Revolution,* 3 vols. (Princeton: The University Library, 1902–7), 2:201–14.

2 The *New-York Mercury*

1. Clarence S. Brigham, *History and Bibliography of American Newspapers, 1690–1820,* 2 vols. (Worcester, Mass.: American Antiquarian Society, 1947), 1:633–35, 699.

2. Beverly McAnear, "James Parker versus William Weyman," *Proceedings of the New Jersey Historical Society* 59 (1941), 3.

3. *New-York Gazette revived in the Weekly Post-Boy,* June 15, 1752.

4. *New-York Mercury,* January 14, 1765.

5. Ibid., November 6, 1752.

6. Ibid., August 31, 1752.

7. Ibid., December 3, 1753. Gaine's Masonic role is sketched in W. K. Walker, "Introducing H. Gaine, Provincial Grand Secretary," American Lodge of Research, Free and Accepted Masons *Transactions* 3, No. 1 (October 31, 1938–October 30, 1939), 11–24.

8. *New-York Mercury,* October 29, 1764.

9. An interesting study of the advertising in the *Mercury* has been made by Elizabeth J. Thompson, "Advertisements of a Moderate Length . . . Five Shillings Each: An Analysis of Advertising in the *New-York Gazette and Weekly Mercury,* 1755–1775." Paper read before the History Division, Association for Education in Journalism, University of Colorado, August 1967.

3 Churchmen and Legislators

1. Dorothy R. Dillon, *The New York Triumvirate* (New York: Columbia University Press, 1949), pp. 32–33.

2. Ibid., p. 33.

3. *New-York Mercury,* September 3, 1753.

4. *The Independent Reflector,* August 30, 1753.

5. *New-York Mercury,* September 3, 1753.

6. *The Occasional Reverberator,* September 4, 1753.

7. *New-York Mercury,* November 13, 1753.

8. New York (Colony), *Journal of the Votes and Proceedings of the General Assembly of the Colony of New York, 1692–1765,* 2 vols. (New York: Hugh Gaine, 1766), 2:358.

9. *New-York Mercury,* November 12, 1753.

10. *Journal of . . . the General Assembly of New York,* 2:358–59.

11. *New-York Mercury,* August 12, 1754; August 19, 1754.

12. Only one copy of one issue of *The Plebean* has survived: No. 5, of September 11, 1754, reprinted in Clarence S. Brigham, *Additions and Corrections to History and Bibliography of American Newspapers, 1690–1820* (Worcester, Mass.: American Antiquarian Society, 1961), p. 24.

4 Printing Away with Amazing Success

1. Paul L. Ford, ed., *The Journals of Hugh Gaine, Printer,* 2 vols. (New York: Dodd, Mead, & Co., 1902), 1:16. Cf. Beverly McAnear, "James Parker versus William Weyman," *Proceedings of the New Jersey Historical Society* 59 (1941), 9.

2. Livingston to Noah Welles, December 7, 1754, quoted in Theodore Sedgwick, Jr., *A Memoir of the Life of William Livingston* (New York: J. & J. Harper, 1833), pp. 104–5.

3. Dorothy R. Dillon, *The New York Triumvirate* (New York: Columbia University Press, 1949), p. 38.

4. *New-York Mercury*, May 12, 1757; May 9, 1763; October 3, 1763.
5. Ibid., September 26, 1757.
6. Ibid., December 20, 1756; May 29, 1758; January 7, 1760.
7. Ibid., May 13, 1765. Cf. ibid., June 2, 1755; May 29, 1758; August 17, 1761.
8. Ibid., August 22, 1757.
9. Ibid., August 14, 1758.
10. Ibid., February 10, 1755.
11. Ibid., March 22, 1762.
12. *New-York Gazette*, September 29, 1760.
13. *New-York Mercury*, May 4, 1761; October 19, 1761; October 26, 1761.

5 Prelude to a Revolution

1. Clarence S. Brigham, *History and Bibliography of American Newspapers, 1690–1820*, 2 vols. (Worcester, Mass.: American Antiquarian Society, 1947), 1:629, 635.
2. Victor H. Palsits, "John Holt—Printer and Postmaster," *Bulletin of the New York Public Library* 24 (1920), 483. Charles R. Hildeburn, *Sketches of Printers and Printing in Colonial New York* (New York: Dodd, Mead and Co., 1895), p. 25.
3. Brigham, *History and Bibliography*, 1:638.
4. Ibid., pp. 607–8, 677.
5. *New-York Mercury*, July 12, 1762; August 23, 1762; February 13, 1764; June 3, 1765.
6. Andrew Burnaby, *Travels in the Middle Settlements in North America, in the Years 1759 and 1761: With Observations Upon the State of the Colonies*, 3d ed., rev. (London: T. Payne, 1798), p. 86.
7. Robert Rogers, *A Concise Account of North America* (1765; reprint ed., New York: Johnson Reprint Corp., 1966), p. 69.
8. Burnaby, p. 118.
9. *New-York Mercury*, January 30, 1764; November 5, 1764; November 12, 1764.
10. Ibid., December 3, 1764; December 31, 1764.
11. Ibid., December 24, 1764.
12. Ibid., October 1, 1764.
13. Ibid.
14. Ibid., April 2, 1764; *New-York Gazette*, April 5, 1764; *New-York Gazette, or the Weekly Post-Boy*, April 5, 1764.

6 No Stamped Paper to be Had

1. Samuel Eliot Morison and Henry Steele Commager, *The Growth of the American Republic*, 2 vols. (New York: Oxford University Press, 1962), 1:159.

2. Ibid.

3. *New-York Mercury*, May 20, 1765; June 17, 1765.

4. *New-York Mercury*, December 23, 1765.

5. Arthur M. Schlesinger, *Prelude to Independence: The Newspaper War on Britain, 1764–1776* (New York: Alfred A. Knopf, 1958), p. 21.

6. *New-York Mercury*, August 19, 1765; August 26, 1765.

7. Ibid., September 2, 1765.

8. Ibid., September 16, 1765; *Weekly Post-Boy*, September 12, 1765.

9. Colden to Sir Jeffrey Amherst, January 13, 1766, *The Colden Letter Books, 1760–1775*, New York Historical Society Collections, vols. 9, 10 (New York: New York Historical Society, 1877–78), 10:91.

10. Colden to the Secretary of State and Board of Trade, December 6, 1765, *The Colden Letter Books*, 10:75.

11. Colden to Henry Seymour Conway, September 23, 1765, *The Colden Letter Books*, 10:36.

12. *New-York Mercury*, October 7, 1765; October 14, 1765; April 7, 1766.

13. Gaine erred in stating the date of the first issue of the *Mercury*; August 8 was the Saturday following the date of issue, August 3, 1752.

14. Isaiah Thomas, *The History of Printing in America*, 2d ed., 2 vols. (Albany, N.Y.: American Antiquarian Society, 1874), 2:107.

15. Colden to Sir Jeffrey Amherst, January 13, 1766, *The Colden Letter Books*, 10:91.

16. Parker to Franklin, May 6, 1766, "Letters from James Parker to Franklin," *Massachusetts Historical Society Proceedings*, Second Series, 16:225.

17. *New-York Mercury*, April 7, 1766.

18. Ibid., January 23, 1764.

19. Ibid., February 7, 1763.

20. Clarence S. Brigham, *History and Bibliography of American Newspapers, 1690–1820*, 2 vols. (Worcester, Mass.: American Antiquarian Society, 1947), 1:656.

21. Ibid., pp. 636, 638.

7 Fair Liberty's Call

1. *New-York Mercury,* August 24, 1767; October 5, 1767.

2. Beverly McAnear, "James Parker versus William Weyman," *Proceedings of the New York Historical Society* 59 (1941), 8–9, 23.

3. Gaine to Sir William Johnson, August 26, 1768, in E. B. O'Callaghan, *The Documentary History of the State of New York,* 4 vols. (Albany: Charles Van Benthuysen, 1851), 4:384. Gaine to Johnson, September 17, 1768, ibid., p. 384.

4. *Journal of the Votes and Proceedings of the General Assembly of the Colony of New York,* 2 vols. (New York: Hugh Gaine, 1764–66), 2:688.

5. Ibid., 74. McAnear, p. 23.

6. Gaine to Johnson, August 26, 1768, O'Callaghan, 4:384–85.

7. William Weyman to the Rev. Dr. Henry Barclay, April 2, 1763, O'Callaghan, 4:326–27. Weyman to Barclay, October 20, 1763, O'Callaghan, 4:334–35. Gaine to Johnson, August 26, 1768, O'Callaghan, 4:384–85. Gaine to Johnson, February 2, 1769, O'Callaghan, 4:405.

8. Dorothy R. Dillon, *The New York Triumvirate* (New York: Columbia University Press, 1949), pp. 43–45.

9. *New-York Mercury,* July 18, 1768; July 25, 1769.

10. John Adams to Jedidiah Morse, December 2, 1815, in *The Works of John Adams,* ed. Charles Francis Adams, 10 vols. (Boston: Little, Brown and Co., 1851–56), 10:185.

11. Adams to Morse, January 1, 1816, *The Works of John Adams,* 10:199.

12. *New-York Mercury,* April 4, 1768.

13. Ibid., April 18, 1768; August 22, 1768.

14. Ibid., September 12, 1768.

15. Ibid., July 18, 1768.

16. Ibid., May 1, 1769.

17. Ibid., December 28, 1767; March 20, 1769.

18. Ibid., May 8, 1769.

19. Ibid., November 14, 1768.

20. Gaine to Johnson, November 19, 1768, O'Callaghan, 4:249. Gaine to Johnson, April 22, 1769, ibid., p. 259.

21. Parker to Franklin, February 2, 1770, "Letters from James Parker to Franklin," *Massachusetts Historical Society Proceedings,* Second Series, 16 (Boston: Massachusetts Historical Society, 1903), 221.

22. *New-York Mercury,* March 7, 1768; July 4, 1768.

23. Ibid., May 29, 1769.
24. Ibid., May 15, 1769.
25. Ibid., July 2, 1770.
26. Ibid., July 16, 1770.
27. Ibid., July 23, 1770; August 6, 1770.

8 Most Shocking Transactions

1. *New-York Mercury,* July 4, 1768.
2. Ibid., July 11, 1768.
3. Ibid., September 26, 1768; October 3, 1768; October 10, 1768.
4. Ibid., March 19, 1770.
5. Ibid., November 21, 1768.
6. [William Smith], *Historical Memoirs,* ed. William H. Sabine, 2 vols. (New York: Colburn & Tegg, 1956–58), 1:46.
7. *New-York Mercury,* January 8, 1770.
8. Ibid., August 13, 1770.
9. Ibid., February 12, 1770.
10. Wilbur C. Abbott, *New York in the American Revolution* (New York: Charles Scribner's Sons, 1929), pp. 87–88.
11. Thomas Jones, *History of New York During the Revolutionary War,* ed. Edward Floyd De Lancey, 2 vols. (New York: Historical Society, 1879), 1:429.
12. *New-York Mercury,* February 19, 1770.
13. Jones, 1:26.
14. *New-York Gazette, or, the Weekly Post-Boy,* February 12, 1770.
15. *New-York Mercury,* April 9, 1770; April 30, 1770; April 23, 1770.
16. Ibid., April 9, 1770.
17. Ibid., April 16, 1770; May 7, 1770; May 14, 1770.
18. Dorothy R. Dillon, *The New York Triumvirate* (New York: Columbia University Press, 1949), p. 121.
19. Parker to Franklin, October 27, 1764, "Letters from James Parker to Franklin," *Massachusetts Historical Society Proceedings,* Second Series, 16 (1903), 193.
20. *New-York Gazette, or, the Weekly Post-Boy,* May 17, 1764. Cf. *Rivington's Royal Gazette,* January 8, 1783.
21. Parker to Franklin, April 23, 1770, "Letters from James Parker to Franklin," p. 225.
22. Parker to Franklin, April 24, 1770, ibid., pp. 225–26. Parker to Franklin, May 10, 1770, ibid., p. 227.

23. Parker to Franklin, February 2, 1770, ibid., p. 221.

24. *New-York Mercury*, July 9, 1770.

9 Tea, but No Sympathy

1. *New-York Mercury*, March 28, 1774.

2. Bernice Marshall, *Colonial Hempstead: Long Island Life Under the Dutch and English*, 2d ed. (Port Washington, N.Y.: Ira J. Friedman, 1962), p. 169.

3. John W. Francis, "Reminiscences of Philip Freneau," *Cyclopedia of American Literature*, ed. E. A. Duyckinck and G. L. Duyckinck, 2 vols. (New York: Charles Scribner, 1855), 1:335.

4. Henry Bamford Parkes, *The American Experience: An Interpretation of the History and Civilization of the American People* (New York: Alfred A. Knopf, 1955), pp. 48–49.

5. Clarence S. Brigham, *History and Bibliography of American Newspapers, 1690–1820*, 2 vols. (Worcester, Mass.: American Antiquarian Society, 1947), 2:782.

6. Ibid., 1:636.

7. Charles A. Beard and Mary R. Beard, *The Rise of American Civilization*, rev. ed. (New York: The Macmillan Co., 1934), pp. 223–24. Cf. Arthur M. Schlesinger, *The Colonial Merchants and the American Revolution, 1763–1776*, 2d ed. (New York: Facsimile Library, Inc., 1939), pp. 262–64.

8. *New-York Mercury*, October 25, 1773.

9. Ibid., December 27, 1773.

10. Cadwallader Colden to the Earl of Dartmouth, September 7, 1774, *The Colden Letter Books, 1760–1775*, New York Historical Society Collections, vols. 9, 10 (New York: New York Historical Society, 1877–78), 10:359–60.

11. *New-York Mercury*, May 23, 1774.

12. Ibid.

13. Ibid., September 26, 1774.

14. Ibid., February 13, 1775.

15. Peter Force, ed., *American Archives, Fourth Series*, 6 vols. (Washington, D.C.: M. St. Clair Clarke and Peter Force, 1837–46), 1:1097–98, 1257–58.

16. *New-York Mercury*, March 6, 1775; April 10, 1775.

17. Ibid., December 19, 1774.

10 Drums, Fifes, and Propaganda—American Manufacture

1. Colden to Gage, May 31, 1775, *The Colden Letter Books, 1760–*

1775, New York Historical Society Collections, vols. 9, 10 (New York: New York Historical Society, 1877–78), 10:414.

2. Ibid.

3. *New-York Mercury,* June 5, 1775.

4. Ibid., August 17, 1761.

5. New York (State), Minutes of the Committee of Observation, May 1, 1775–January 15, 1776, Peter Force Transcripts, Library of Congress.

6. *New-York Mercury,* August 28, 1775; October 6, 1775; December 4, 1775; January 15, 1776.

7. Ibid., October 23, 1775.

8. Ibid., March 18, 1776.

9. Ibid., March 20, 1775.

10. Peter Force, ed., *American Archives, Fourth Series,* 6 vols. (Washington, D.C.: M. St. Clair Clarke and Peter Force, 1837–46), 2:12–13, 132.

11. Ibid., pp. 836–37, 899–900, 1284.

12. Joseph Galloway, *A Candid Examination of the Mutual Claims of Great-Britain and the Colonies: With a Plan of Accomodation on Constitutional Principles* (London: G. Wilkie and R. Foulder, 1780), pp. v–vi.

13. Clarence S. Brigham, *History and Bibliography of American Newspapers, 1690–1820,* 2 vols. (Worcester, Mass.: American Antiquarian Society, 1947), 1:675. Charles R. Hildeburn, *Sketches of Printers and Printing in Colonial New York* (New York: Dodd, Mead, and Co., 1895), pp. 153–54.

14. Thomas Jones, *History of New York During the Revolutionary War,* ed. Edward Floyd De Lancey, 2 vols. (New York: Historical Society, 1879), 1:64–65.

15. Ibid., p. 65.

16. Force, *American Archives, Fourth Series,* 5:439.

17. Arthur M. Schlesinger, *Prelude to Independence: The Newspaper War on Britain* (New York: Alfred A. Knopf, 1958), p. 251.

18. Ibid., p. 261.

19. *New-York Mercury,* March 25, 1776.

20. Ibid., April 8, 1776.

21. Ibid., April 22, 1776; April 29, 1776; May 6, 1776.

22. Ibid., June 10, 1776; June 17, 1776; June 24, 1776.

23. R. W. G. Vail, "The Unique *Declaration of Independence* Printed by Hugh Gaine," *New York Historical Society Quarterly* 32 (1948), 224.

24. *New-York Mercury,* July 15, 1776.
25. Force, *American Archives, Fourth Series,* 1:1432.
26. Wilbur C. Abbott, *New York in the American Revolution* (New York: Charles Scribner's Sons, 1929), p. 158.
27. *New-York Mercury,* September 9, 1776.
28. Gaine to Varick, September 8, 1776, *The Journals of Hugh Gaine, Printer,* ed. Paul L. Ford, 2 vols. (New York: Dodd, Mead & Co., 1902), 1:54.
29. *New-York Mercury* (Newark), September 21, 1776.

11 Patriot in Newark

1. Edward H. Tatum, Jr., ed., *The American Journal of Ambrose Serle, Secretary to Lord Howe, 1776–1778* (San Marino, Calif.: The Huntington Library, 1940), p. 113.
2. Ibid., pp. xxi, xiii–xiv.
3. Ibid., p. 114.
4. Serle to Lord Dartmouth, November 26, 1776, in Benjamin F. Stevens, ed., *Facsimiles of Manuscripts in European Archives Relating to America, 1773–1783,* 25 vols. (London: Chiswick Press, 1889–98), 24, no. 2046.
5. Lord George Germain to William Knox, June 24, 1777, Great Britain, Historical Manuscripts Commission, *Report on Manuscripts in Various Collections,* 8 vols. (London: Her Majesty's Stationery Office, 1901–13), 6:131.
6. *New-York Mercury* (New York), September 3, 1753.
7. Ibid., February 10, 1777–April 7, 1777.
8. Tatum, p. 185.
9. *New-York Mercury* (New York), February 10, 1777.
10. Tatum, p. 187.
11. Serle to Dartmouth, November 26, 1776, Stevens's *Facsimiles,* no. 2046.
12. Gaine to Varick, September 8, 1776, *The Journals of Hugh Gaine, Printer,* ed. Paul L. Ford, 2 vols. (New York: Dodd, Mead, & Co., 1902), 1:54.
13. *Gaine's Universal Register, or, American and British Kalendar, for the Year 1777* (New York: Hugh Gaine, 1777), p. 83.
14. *New-York Mercury* (New York), October 28, 1776.
15. Nicholas Cresswell, *The Journals of Nicholas Cresswell* (New York: The Dial Press, 1924), p. 159.
16. *The Kemble Papers,* New York Historical Society Collections, vols.

16, 17 (New York: New York Historical Society, 1884–85), 16:91–92.

17. Tatum, p. 135.

12 With the Redcoats

1. Bernard Mason, *The Road to Independence: The Revolutionary Movement in New York, 1773–1777* (Lexington: University of Kentucky Press, 1966), p. 106.

2. Paul L. Ford, ed., *The Journals of Hugh Gaine, Printer,* 2 vols. (New York: Dodd, Mead & Co., 1902), 2:70.

3. Edward H. Tatum, Jr., ed., *The American Journal of Ambrose Serle, Secretary to Lord Howe, 1776–1778* (San Marino, Calif.: The Huntington Library, 1940), p. 113.

4. Tatum, p. 135.

5. *New-York Mercury* (Newark), November 2, 1776.

6. Robert Donkin, *Military Collections and Remarks* (New York: Hugh Gaine, 1777), p. iii.

7. Ibid., p. 123.

8. Ibid., p. 190.

9. *Pennsylvania Journal,* February 19, 1777.

10. Ibid., April 30, 1777.

11. Philip S. Foner, ed., *The Complete Writings of Thomas Paine,* 2 vols. (New York: The Citadel Press, 1945), 1:71.

12. Tatum, p. 219.

13. Serle to Lord Dartmouth, November 26, 1776, in Benjamin F. Stevens, ed., *Facsimiles of Manuscripts in European Archives Relating to America, 1773–1783,* 25 vols. (London: Chiswick Press, 1889–98), 24, no. 2046.

14. Ford, 2:50–51.

15. Frank Luther Mott, *American Journalism: A History of Newspapers in the United States Through 260 Years, 1690–1950,* rev. ed. (New York: The Macmillan Co., 1950), p. 86.

16. New York (State), Minutes of the Committee of Safety, January 22, 1777, New York Records, Convention I, Revolution 1777, Peter Force Transcripts, Library of Congress.

17. Ibid., January 31, 1777.

18. Parker to Franklin, February 2, 1770, "Letters from James Parker to Franklin," *Massachusetts Historical Society Proceedings,* Second Series, 16 (1903), 221.

19. Clarence S. Brigham, *History and Bibliography of American News-*

papers, 1690–1820, 2 vols. (Worcester, Mass.: American Antiquarian Society, 1947), 1:613, 688, 664.

20. S. G. W. Benjamin, "Notable Editors Between 1776 and 1800," *Magazine of American History* 17 (1887), 101–3. Cf. Isaiah Thomas, *The History of Printing in America,* 2d ed. (Albany, N.Y.: American Antiquarian Society, 1974).

21. Tatum, p. 283.

22. William Dunlap, *A History of the American Theatre* (New York: J & J Harper, 1832), p. 49.

23. Deposition of Adam Burger, November 20, 1776, enclosure to letter, Thomas Mifflin to Robert Morris, November 21, 1776, *Revolutionary Papers,* New York Historical Society Collections, vols. 11, 12, 13 (New York: New York Historical Society, 1879–81), 11:407.

24. Washington to Henry Laurens, April 23, 1778, *The Writings of George Washington,* ed. Jared Sparks, 12 vols. (Boston: American Stationers Co.; J. B. Russell, 1834–37), 5:336. Laurens to Washington, April 27, 1778, *Letters of Members of the Continental Congress,* ed. Edmund C. Burnett, 8 vols. (Washington, D.C.: The Carnegie Institution of Washington, 1921–36), 3:191.

25. Ford, 2:52, 58.

26. Tatum, p. 176.

27. William Heath to George Washington, December 10, 1776, in Peter Force, ed., *American Archives, Fifth Series,* 3 vols. (Washington, D.C.: M. St. Clair and Peter Force, 1848–53), 3:1490.

28. McDougall to Washington, December 30, 1776, *American Archives, Fifth Series,* 3:1490.

29. Ford, 2:70, 93, 145, 152.

30. Dunlap, p. 37.

31. *New-York Mercury,* January 27, 1777.

32. Ibid., January 3, 1780; May 15, 1780; November 6, 1780; February 3, 1783; March 6, 1780.

33. Brigham, *History and Bibliography,* 1:686.

13 A Printer of Good Reputation

1. Clarence S. Brigham, *History and Bibliography of American Newspapers, 1690–1820,* 2 vols. (Worcester, Mass.: American Antiquarian Society, 1947), 1:630, 645, 651, 620, 675, 651.

2. S. G. W. Benjamin, "Notable Editors Between 1776 and 1800 — Influence of the Early American Press," *Magazine of American History* 17 (1887), 127.

3. John W. Francis, "Reminiscences of Christopher Colles," *The Knickerbocker Gallery* (New York: Samuel Hueston, 1885), p. 203.

4. Loudon to Clinton, [?], Paul L. Ford, ed., *The Journals of Hugh Gaine, Printer*, 2 vols. (New York: Dodd, Mead, & Co., 1902), 2:25.

5. William L. Stone, *The History of New York City from the Discovery to the Present Day* (New York: Virtue & Yorston, 1872), p. 287.

6. Ford, 1:66; 2:171, 199.

7. Gaine to [?], May 14, 1806, Ford, 2:225.

8. Ibid., p. 173.

9. Ibid., p. 197.

10. John W. Francis, *Old New York; or, Reminiscences of the Past Sixty Years* (New York: W. J. Middleton, 1865), p. 118.

11. Ibid., pp. 118–19.

12. John W. Francis, "Reminiscences of Philip Freneau," *Cyclopedia of American Literature*, ed. E. A. Duyckinck and G. L. Duyckinck, 2 vols. (New York: Charles Scribner, 1855), 1:335.

13. George O. Seilhamer, *History of the American Theatre From 1774 to 1797*, 3 vols. (New York: Frances P. Harper, 1896), 2:25–26.

14. John Hodgkinson, *A Narrative of his Connection with the Old American Company* (New York: J. Oram, 1797).

15. William Dunlap, *A History of the American Theatre* (New York: J. & J. Harper, 1832), p. 151.

16. *The Diary of William Dunlap* (1776–1839), New York Historical Society Collections, vols. 62, 63, 64 (New York: New York Historical Society, 1930–32), 62:43, 59.

17. Dunlap, *History of the American Theatre*, p. 221.

18. Ford, 1:67–68.

19. *New York Commercial Advertiser*, March 10, 1807.

20. *New York Journal*, April 22, 1790.

21. Ford, 1:65.

22. *Columbian Centinel*, May 2, 1807; *New York Evening Post*, April 26, 1807.

23. Frank Luther Mott, *American Journalism: A History of Newspapers in the United States through 260 Years, 1690–1950*, rev. ed. (New York: The Macmillan Co., 1950), p. 86.

24. Edwin Emery, *The Press and America: An Interpretative History of Journalism*, 2d ed. (Englewood Cliffs, N.J.: Prentice-Hall, Inc., 1962), p. 119.

25. George H. Payne, *History of Journalism in the United States* (New York: D. Appleton & Co., 1920), p. 127.

26. James Grant Wilson, ed., *The Memorial History of the City of New York,* 4 vols. (New York: New-York History Co., 1893), 4:137.

27. Vernon L. Parrington, *Main Currents in American Thought,* 2 vols. (New York: Harcourt, Brace and Co., 1927), 1:189.

28. Carl L. Becker, *Beginnings of the American People* (Ithaca, N.Y.: Great Seal Books, 1963), p. 232.

29. Leonard W. Labaree, "The Nature of American Loyalism," *American Antiquarian Society Proceedings* 54 (1945), 17.

30. Ibid., p. 22.

31. Henry Bramford Parkes, *The American Experience: An Interpretation of the History and Civilization of the American People* (New York: Alfred A. Knopf, 1955), pp. 99–100.

Bibliography

MANUSCRIPTS

Anon. Diary. September 15, 1775–August 12, 1776. Manuscript Division, Library of Congress.

Force Transcripts. Manuscript Division, Library of Congress.

Gaine File. New Jersey Historical Society.

Gaine File. Miscellaneous Collections. Manuscript Division, New York Public Library.

Rivington File. Miscellaneous Collections. Manuscript Division, New York Public Library.

Thompson, Elizabeth J. "Advertisements of a Moderate Length . . . Five Shillings Each: An Analysis of Advertising in the New-York Gazette and Weekly Mercury, 1755–1775." Paper read before the History Division, Association for Education in Journalism, University of Colorado, August, 1967. Mimeographed.

Register of Baptisms in the Parish of Trinity Church, New York. 3 vols. Trinity Church, New York.

Register of Burials in the Parish of Trinity Church, New York. 3 vols. Trinity Church, New York.

Register of Marriages in the Parish of Trinity Church, New York. 3 vols. Trinity Church, New York.

Trinity Vaults Records. Trinity Church, New York.

Vail, Christopher. Journal, 1775–1781. Manuscript Division, Library of Congress.

COLONIAL NEWSPAPERS

The *New-York Gazette, and the Weekly Mercury* was published with the title *New-York Mercury* from August 3, 1752 through

January 25, 1768, and with the full title from February 1, 1768 through November 10, 1783. The earliest available issue is that of August 31, 1752. A bound file of the newspaper is available at the New York Public Library. Numerous libraries possess microfilm copies, which are obtainable through the Inter-Library Loan service.

For bibliographical information on the other newspapers mentioned in the text see Clarence S. Brigham, *History and Bibliography of American Newspapers: 1690–1820,* below under Journalism and Printing Histories.

PUBLISHED LETTERS, DIARIES, CONTEMPORARY RECORDS

Adams, Charles Francis, ed. *The Works of John Adams, Second President of the United States.* 10 vols. Boston: Little, Brown and Co., 1851–56.

Benson, Adolph B., ed. *Peter Kalm's Travels in North America.* 2 vols. New York: Wilson-Erickson, Inc., 1937.

Burke, Edmund. *An Account of the European Settlements in America.* 2 vols. London: R. and J. Dodsley, 1757.

Burnaby, Andrew. *Travels Through the Middle Settlements in North America, in the Years 1759 and 1760; with Observations Upon the State of the Colonies.* 3d ed., rev. London: T. Payne, 1798.

Burnett, Edmund C., ed. *Letters of Members of the Continental Congress.* 8 vols. Washington: The Carnegie Institution of Washington, 1921–36.

The Colden Letter Books, 1760–1775. New York Historical Society Collections, vols. 9, 10. New York: New York Historical Society, 1877–78.

Cresswell, Nicholas. *The Journal of Nicholas Cresswell.* New York: The Dial Press, 1924.

Diary of William Dunlap (1766–1839): The Memoirs of a Dramatist, Theatrical Manager, Painter, Critic, Novelist, and Historian. New York Historical Society Collections, vols. 62, 63, 64. New York: New York Historical Society, 1930–32.

Dorson, Richard, ed. *America Rebels: Narratives of the Patriots.* New York: Pantheon, 1953.

Dunlap, William. *A History of the American Theatre.* New York: J. & J. Harper, 1832.

————. *History of the New Netherlands, Province of New York, and State of New York, to the Adoption of the Federal Constitution.* 2 vols. New York: Carter & Thorp, 1839–40.

Foner, Philip S., ed. *The Complete Writings of Thomas Paine.* 2 vols. New York: The Citadel Press, 1945.

Force, Peter, ed. *American Archives: Fifth Series.* 3 vols. Washington: M. St. Clair and Peter Force, 1848–53.

————. *American Archives: Fourth Series.* 6 vols. Washington: M. St. Clair and Peter Force, 1837–46.

Ford, Paul Leicester, ed. *The Journals of Hugh Gaine, Printer.* 2 vols. New York: Dodd, Mead & Co., 1902.

Francis, John W. *Old New York: or, Reminiscences of the Past Sixty Years.* With a memoir of the author by Henry T. Tuckerman. New York: W. J. Middleton, 1865.

————. "Reminiscences of Christopher Colles." In *The Knickerbocker Gallery.* New York: Samuel Hueston, 1855.

————. "Reminiscences of Philip Freneau." In *Cyclopedia of American Literature,* edited by E. A. Duyckinck and G. L. Duyckinck 2 vols. 1: 327–48. New York: Charles Scribner, 1855.

Freneau, Philip. "Hugh Gaine's Life." *The Freeman's Journal: or, The North American Intelligencer* (Philadelphia), January 8, January 29, February 12, 1783.

[Gaine, Hugh]. *Gaine's Universal Register, or, American and British Kalendar for the Year 1777.* New York: H. Gaine, 1777.

Galloway, Joseph. *A Candid Examination of the Mutual Claims of Great-Britain and the Colonies: With a Plan of Accomodation on Constitutional Principles.* London: G. Wilkie and R. Foulder, 1780.

Hodgkinson, John. *A Narrative of His Connection With the Old American Company, From the Fifth of September, 1792, to the Thirty-first of March, 1797.* New York: J. Oram, 1797.

Jones, Thomas. *History of New York During the Revolutionary War, and of the Leading Events in the Other Colonies at That Period.* Edited by Edward Floyd De Lancey. 2 vols. New York: Printed for the Historical Society, 1879.

The Kemble Papers. New York Historical Society Collections, vols. 16, 17. New York: New York Historical Society, 1884–85.

"Letters from James Parker to Franklin," *Massachusetts Historical*

Society Proceedings, Second Series 16 (Boston: Massachusetts Historical Society, 1903), 186–232.

Longworth's American Almanack, New York Register, and City Directory for the Twenty-Fourth Year of American Independence. New York: John C. Totten and Co., 1799.

Mereness, Newton D, ed. *Travels in the American Colonies.* New York: Antiquarian Press, Ltd., 1961.

O'Callaghan, E. B., ed. *The Documentary History of the State of New-York.* 4 vols. Albany: Weed, Parsons and Co., 1850–51; Charles Van Benthuysen, 1851.

————. *Documents Relative to the Colonial History of the State of New York.* 11 vols. Albany: Weed, Parsons and Co., 1856–61.

Padelford, Philip, ed. *Colonial Panorama, 1775: Dr. Robert Honyman's Journal for March and April.* San Marino, Calif.: The Huntington Library, 1939.

Pattee, Fred Lewis, ed. *The Poems of Philip Freneau, Poet of the American Revolution.* 3 vols. Princeton: The University Library, 1902–7.

Revolutionary Papers. New York Historical Society *Collections,* vols. 11, 12, 13. New York: New York Historical Society, 1879–81.

Rogers, Robert. *A Concise Account of North America.* Reprint. New York: Johnson Reprint Corporation, 1966.

Seeber, Edward D., trans. *On the Threshold of Liberty: Journal of a Frenchman's Tour of the American Colonies in 1777.* Bloomington: Indiana University Press, 1959.

[Smith, William]. *Historical Memoirs.* Edited by William H. W. Sabine. 2 vols. New York: Colburn & Tegg, 1956–58.

————. *The History of the Province of New York From the First Discovery to the Year 1732.* London: Thomas Wilcox, 1757.

Sparks, Jared, ed. *Correspondence of the American Revolution.* Boston: Little, Brown, and Co., 1853.

————, ed. *The Writings of George Washington.* 12 vols. Boston: American Stationers' Co.; J. B. Russell [etc.], 1834–37.

Stevens, Benjamin F., ed. *Facsimiles of Manuscripts in European Archives Relating to America, 1773–1783.* 25 vols. London: Chiswick Press, 1889–98.

Syrett, Harold C., and Cooke, Jacob E., eds. *The Papers of Alexander*

Hamilton. 13 vols. New York: Columbia University Press, 1961–67.

Tatum, Edward H., Jr., ed. *The American Journal of Ambrose Serle.* San Marino, Calif.: The Huntington Library, 1940.

Thomas, Ebenezer Smith. *Reminiscences of the Last Sixty-Five Years, Commencing with the Battle of Lexington.* 2 vols. Hartford: Case, Tiffany and Burnham, 1840.

Thomas, Isaiah. *The History of Printing in America.* 2d ed. Albany, N.Y.: American Antiquarian Society, 1874.

Van Schaack, Henry Cruger. *The Life of Peter Van Schaak, LLD, Embracing Selections From His Correspondence and Other Writings During the American Revolution and His Exile in England.* New York: D. Appleton & Co., 1842.

PUBLIC DOCUMENTS

Great Britain. Historical Manuscripts Commission. *Report on American Manuscripts in the Royal Institution of Great Britain.* 4 vols. London: His Majesty's Stationery Office, 1904–9.

———. *American Papers. The Manuscripts of the Earl of Dartmouth,* vol. 2: London: Her Majesty's Stationery Office, 1895.

———. *Report on Manuscripts in Various Collections.* 8 vols. London: His Majesty's Stationery Office, 1901–14.

New York (Colony). *Journal of the Votes and Proceedings of the General Assembly of the Colony of New York. Began the 8th Day of November, 1743; and Ended the 23d of December, 1765.* 2 vols. New York: Hugh Gaine, 1764–66.

New York (State). *Journals of the Provincial Congress, 1775–1777.* 2 vols. Albany, N.Y.: Weed, Parsons and Co., 1842.

U.S. Continental Congress. *Journals of the Continental Congress, 1774–1789.* Washington: Government Printing Office, 1904–37.

PERIOD AND GENERAL HISTORIES, BIOGRAPHIES

Abbott, Wilbur C. *New York in the American Revolution.* New York and London: Charles Scribner's Sons, 1929.

Andrews, Charles M. *The Colonial Background of the American Revolution.* Rev. ed. New Haven: Yale University Press, 1931.

Barck, Dorothy C. "A List of 500 Inhabitants of New York City in 1775 with Their Occupations and Addresses." *New-York Historical Society Quarterly Bulletin* 23 (1939), 23–31.

Barck, Oscar T. *New York City During the War for Independence.* Port Washington, N.Y.: I. J. Friedman, 1966.

Beard, Charles A., and Beard, Mary R. *The Rise of American Civilization.* Rev. ed. (2 vols. in 1). New York: The Macmillan Co., 1934.

Becker, Carl L. *The Eve of the Revolution.* New Haven: Yale University Press, 1918.

———. *The History of Political Parties in the Province of New York.* Madison: The University of Wisconsin Press, 1960.

Beekman, Fenwick. "The Origin of 'Bellevue' Hospital as Shown in the New York City Health Committee Minutes During the Yellow Fever Epidemics of 1793–95." *New-York Historical Society Quarterly* 37 (1953), 205–27.

Bradsher, Earl L. *Matthew Carey, Editor, Author and Publisher: A Study in American Literary Development.* New York: Columbia University Press, 1912.

Coad, Oral S. *William Dunlap: A Study of His Life and Works and of His Place in Contemporary Culture.* New York: Russell & Russell, 1962.

Cortelyou, Irwin F., and Theodore Bolton. "References to Paintings in the Account Books (1790–1834) of Ezra Ames." *New-York Historical Society Quarterly* 35 (1951), 15–53.

Crosby, Ernest H. "The Rutgers Family of New York." *New York Genealogical and Biographical Record* 17 (1886), 82–93.

Cross, A. L. *The Anglican Episcopate and the American Colonies.* New York: Longmans, Green and Co., 1902.

Curti, Merle E. *The Growth of American Thought.* 3d ed. New York: Harper & Row, 1964.

Dillon, Dorothy R. *The New York Triumvirate.* New York: Columbia University Press, 1949.

Fleming, Reverend Frederic S. "The Two Hundred and Fiftieth Anniversary of the Parish of Trinity Church in the City of New York." *New-York Historical Society Quarterly* 31 (1947), 78–87.

Flick, Alexander C., ed. *History of the State of New York.* 10 vols.

1933–37. Reprint. (10 vols. in 5) Port Washington, N.Y.: Ira J. Friedman, Inc., 1962.

———. *Loyalism in New York During the American Revolution.* New York: Columbia University Press, 1901.

Gipson, Lawrence H. *The Coming of the Revolution, 1763–1775.* New York: Harper and Bros., 1954.

Greene, Evarts B. *The Revolutionary Generation, 1763–1790. A History of American Life*, vol. 4. Edited by Arthur M. Schlesinger and Dixon Ryan Fox. New York: The Macmillan Co., 1943.

Harrington, Virginia D. *The New York Merchant on the Eve of the Revolution.* New York: Columbia University Press, 1935.

Hildreth, Richard. *The History of the United States of America from the Discovery of the Continent to the Organization of Government Under the Federal Constitution.* Rev. ed. 6 vols. New York: Harper and Bros., 1880.

Jameson, J. Franklin. *The American Revolution Considered as a Social Movement.* Princeton: Princeton University Press, 1926.

"John Adams, Knox and Washington." *American Antiquarian Society Proceedings* 56 (Worcester, Mass.: American Antiquarian Society, 1947), 207–38.

Keep, Austin B. *History of the New York Society Library.* New York: The DeVinne Press, 1908.

Labaree, Leonard W. "The Nature of American Loyalism." *American Antiquarian Society Proceedings* 54 (Worcester, Mass.: American Antiquarian Society, 1945), 15–58.

Lamb, Martha J. *History of the City of New York.* 2 vols. New York and Chicago: A. S. Barnes and Co., 1877–80.

Lecky, William E. H. *The American Revolution, 1763–1783.* Arranged and edited with historical and bibliographical notes by James Albert Woodburn. New York: D. Appleton, 1898.

———. *A History of Ireland in the Eighteenth Century.* 5 vols. London and Bombay: Longmans, Green, and Co., 1906–9.

Lemisch, L. Jesse. "New York's Petitions and Resolves of December 1765: Liberals vs. Radicals." *New-York Historical Society Quarterly* 49 (1965), 313–26.

Lydekker, John Wolfe. *The Life and Letters of Charles Inglis.* London: Society for Promoting Christian Knowledge, 1936.

Machesy, Piers. *The War for America, 1775–1783*. Cambridge: Harvard University Press, 1964.

Main, Jackson T. *Rebel Versus Tory: The Crisis of the Revolution.* Chicago: Rand-McNally, 1963.

Marshall, Bernice. *Colonial Hempstead: Long Island Life Under the Dutch and English.* 2d ed. Port Washington, N.Y.: Ira J. Friedman, Inc., 1962.

Mason, Bernard. *The Road to Independence: The Revolutionary Movement in New York, 1773–1777.* Lexington: University of Kentucky Press, 1966.

Merritt, Richard L. *Symbols of American Community, 1735–1775.* New Haven: Yale University Press, 1966.

Miller, John C. *Origins of the American Revolution.* Boston: Little, Brown and Co., 1943.

Moore, Frank. *The Diary of the Revolution.* Hartford: J. B. Buer, 1876.

Morgan, Edmund S., and Morgan, Helen M. *The Stamp Act Crisis: Prologue to Revolution.* Chapel Hill: University of North Carolina Press, 1953.

Morison, Samuel Eliot. *The Oxford History of the American People.* New York: Oxford University Press, 1965.

———, and Commager, Henry Steele. *The Growth of the American Republic.* 2 vols. New York: Oxford University Press, 1962.

Morris, Richard B. *The Era of the American Revolution.* New York: Columbia University Press, 1939.

Nelson, William H. *The American Tory.* Oxford: The Clarendon Press, 1961.

Parkes, Henry Bamford. *The American Experience: An Interpretation of the History and Civilization of the American People.* New York: Alfred A. Knopf, 1955.

Parrington, Vernon L. *Main Currents in American Thought.* 3 vols. New York: Harcourt, Brace and Co., 1927–30.

"Revolutionary New York." *New-York Historical Society Quarterly Bulletin* 42 (1933), 17–18.

Rossiter, Clinton L. *The First American Revolution: The American Colonies on the Eve of Independence.* New York: Harcourt, Brace and Co., 1956.

Sabine, Lorenzo. *Biographical Sketches of Loyalists of the American*

Revolution with an Historical Essay. 2 vols. Port Washington, N.Y.: Kennikat Press, Inc., 1966.

———. *An Historical Essay on the Loyalists of the American Revolution.* Springfield, Mass.: Walden Press, 1957.

Savelle, Max. *A History of Colonial America.* Revised and edited by Robert Middlekauff. New York: Holt, Rinehart and Winston, 1964.

Schlesinger, Arthur Meier. *The Colonial Merchants and the American Revolution: 1763–1776.* New York: Facsimile Library, Inc., 1939.

———. *New Viewpoints in American History.* New York: The Macmillan Co., 1925.

Sedgwick, Theodore, Jr. *A Memoir of the Life of William Livingston.* New York: J. & J. Harper, 1833.

Seilhamer, George O. *History of the American Theatre, From 1774 to 1797.* 3 vols. New York: Francis P. Harper, 1896.

Simpson, Sarah H. J. "The Federal Procession in the City of New York." *New-York Historical Society Quarterly Bulletin,* 9 (1925), 39–57.

"Stamp Activities in New York, 1765." *New-York Historical Society Quarterly Bulletin* 5 (1921), 45–57.

Still, Bayrd. *Mirror for Gotham: New York as Seen by Contemporaries from Dutch Days to the Present.* New York: University Press, 1956.

Stokes, I. N. P. *The Iconography of Manhattan Island.* 6 vols. New York: Robert H. Dodd, 1895–1928.

Stone, William L. *The History of New York City from the Discovery to the Present Day.* New York: Virtue & Yorston, 1872.

Thomas, Milton H. "John Kemp." In *Dictionary of American Biography,* edited by Allen Johnson and Dumas Malone. 11 vols., 5:319–20. New York: Charles Scribner's Sons, 1960.

———. "The King's College Building, with Some Notes on Its Later Tenants." *New-York Historical Society Quarterly* 39 (1955), 23–60.

Trevelyan, George Otto. *The American Revolution.* 3 vols. London and New York: Longmans, Green and Co., 1905.

———. *George the Third and Charles Fox.* 2 vols. New York: Longmans, Green and Co., 1912–14.

Tyler, Moses C. *The Literary History of the American Revolution,*
1763–1783. 2 vols. New York: G. P. Putnam's Sons, 1957.

Vail, R. W. G. "The Loyalist Declaration of Dependence of November 28, 1776." *New-York Historical Society Quarterly* 31
(1947), 68–71.

Van Tyne, Claude H. *The Causes of the War of Independence.* Boston:
Houghton Mifflin Co., 1922.

———. *The Loyalists in the American Revolution.* New York: The
Macmillan Co., 1902.

Wall, Alexander J. "New York and the *Declaration of Independence.*"
New-York Historical Society Quarterly Bulletin 10 (1926),
43–51.

Warfel, Harry R., Gabriel, Ralph H., and Williams, Stanley, eds. *The*
American Mind. New York: American Book Co., 1937.

Weeks, Lyman Horace. *A History of Paper-Manufacturing in the*
United States, 1690–1916. New York: Lockwood Trade Journal
Co., 1916.

Wertenbaker, Thomas J. *Father Knickerbocker Rebels: New York City*
During the Revolution. New York: Charles Scribner's Sons,
1948.

Wilson, James Grant, ed. *The Memorial History of the City of New-*
York. 4 vols. New York: New-York History Co., 1893.

Wilson, Woodrow. *A History of the American People.* 5 vols. New
York: Harper and Bros., 1902.

Winsor, Justin. *The United States of North America. Narrative and*
Critical History of America. Vol. 6. Boston and New York:
Houghton Mifflin and Co., 1888.

Wright, Esmond. *Causes and Consequences of the American Revolu-*
tion. Chicago: Quadrangle Books, 1966.

Wright, Louis B. *The Cultural Life of the American Colonies, 1607–*
1763. New York: Harper, 1957.

JOURNALISM AND PRINTING HISTORIES, BIBLIOGRAPHIES,
BIOGRAPHIES

Benjamin, S. G. W. "Notable Editors Between 1776 and 1800 — Influence of the Early American Press." *Magazine of American*
History 17 (1887), 97–127.

———. "A Group of Pre-Revolutionary Editors." *Magazine of American History* 17 (1887), 1–28.

Bennett, Henry Leigh. "Ambrose Serle." In *The Dictionary of National Biography,* edited by Sir Leslie Stephen and Sir Sidney Lee. 22 vols., Rev. ed., 17:1192. London: Oxford University Press, 1959–60.

Bleyer, Willard G. *Main Currents in the History of American Journalism.* Boston: Houghton, Mifflin Co., 1927.

Brigham, Clarence S. *Additions and Corrections to History and Bibliography of American Newspapers: 1690–1820.* Worcester, Mass.: American Antiquarian Society, 1961.

———. *History and Bibliography of American Newspapers: 1690–1820.* 2 vols. Worcester, Mass.: American Antiquarian Society, 1947.

———. *Journals and Journeymen: A Contribution to the History of Early American Newspapers.* Philadelphia: University of Pennsylvania Press, 1950.

Buckingham, Joseph T. *Specimens of Newspaper Literature.* 2 vols. Boston: Redding and Co., 1850.

Cheever, Lawrence Oakley. *Hugh Gaine, Printer.* Muscatine, Iowa: The Prairie Press, 1943.

Davidson, Philip G. *Propaganda and the American Revolution: 1763–1783.* Chapel Hill: The University of North Carolina Press, 1941.

———. "Whig Propagandists and the American Revolution." *American Historical Review* 39 (1934), 442–53.

D'Innocenzo, Michael, and Turner, John J., Jr. "The Role of New York Newspapers in the Stamp Act Crisis, 1764–66." *New-York Historical Society Quarterly* 51 (1967), 215–31, 345–65.

Emery, Edwin. *The Press and America: An Interpretative History of Journalism.* 2d ed. Englewood Cliffs, N.J.: Prentice-Hall, Inc., 1962.

Hewlett, Leroy. "James Rivington, Tory Printer." In *Books in America's Past: Essays Honoring Rudolph H. Gjelsness,* edited by David Kaser, pp. 166–93. Charlottesville, Va.: The University of Virginia Press, 1966.

Hudson, Frederic. *Journalism in the United States from 1690 to 1872.* New York: Harper and Bros., 1873.

"Hugh Gaine, Irishman, Publisher." *The Recorder* 1 (1902), 1.

Jones, Robert W. *Journalism in the United States.* New York: E. P. Dutton and Co., Inc., 1947.

Klapper, August. *The Printer in Eighteenth-Century Williamsburg. An Account of his Life & Times, his Office, & his Craft.* Williamsburg Craft Series. Williamsburg: Colonial Williamsburg, 1964.

Kobre, Sidney. *Development of American Journalism.* Dubuque: William C. Brown Co., 1969.

——. *The Development of the Colonial Newspaper.* Pittsburgh: Colonial Press, Inc., 1944.

——. *Foundations of American Journalism.* Tallahassee: Florida State University, 1958.

——. "The Revolutionary Colonial Press—A Social Interpretation." *Journalism Quarterly* 20 (1943), 193–97.

Lee, A. M. "Pioneer American Daily in 1783." *Editor & Publisher,* March 10, 1934, p. 37.

——. *The Daily Newspaper in America: the Evolution of a Social Instrument.* New York: The Macmillan Co., 1937.

Lee, James Melvin. *History of American Journalism.* Boston and New York: Houghton Mifflin Co., 1917.

Levy, Leonard W. "Did the Zenger Case Really Matter." *William and Mary Quarterly,* 3d Series, 17 (1960), 35–50.

——. *Freedom of Speech and Press in Early American History: Legacy of Suppression.* New York: Harper & Row, Harper Torchbooks, 1963.

McAnear, Beverly. "James Parker versus William Weyman." *New Jersey Historical Society Proceedings* 59 (1941), 1–23.

McKay, George L., comp. "A Register of Artists, Booksellers, Printers and Publishers in New York City, 1781–1800." *Bulletin of the New York Public Library* 45 (1941), 387–95, 483–99.

McMurtrie, Douglas C. *The Beginnings of the American Newspaper.* Chicago: Black Cat Press, 1935.

——. *A History of Printing in the United States.* 2 vols. New York: R. R. Bowker Co., 1936.

Martin, C. M., and Martin, B. E. "The New York Press and Its Makers in the Eighteenth Century." In *Historic New York.* 2 vols., 2:121–62. New York and London: G. P. Putnam's Sons, 1899.

Mott, Frank Luther. *American Journalism: A History of Newspapers in the United States Through 260 Years, 1690–1950.* Rev. ed. New York: The Macmillan Co., 1950.

Munsell, Joel. *The Typographical Miscellany.* Albany: Joel Munsell, 1850.

Munter, Robert. *The History of the Irish Newspaper, 1685–1765.* Cambridge: The University Press, 1967.

Nelson, William. "The American Newspapers of the Eighteenth Century as Sources of History." In *Annual Report of the American Historical Association for the Year 1908.* 2 vols., 1:211–22. Washington: Government Printing Office.

———. "Some New Jersey Printers and Printing in the Eighteenth Century." *American Antiquarian Society Proceedings,* New Series, 21 (Worcester, Mass.: American Antiquarian Society, 1911), 15–56.

Oswald, John Clyde. *Printing in the Americas.* New York: The Gregg Publishing Co., 1937.

Paine, Nathaniel, ed. "Early American Broadsides, 1680–1800." *American Antiquarian Society Proceedings,* 11 (Worcester, Mass.: American Antiquarian Society, 1898), 455–516.

Paltsits, Vernon H. "Hugh Gaine." In *Dictionary of American Biography,* edited by Allen Johnson and Dumas Malone. 11 vols., 4:91–92. New York: Charles Scribner's Sons, 1960.

———. "John Holt, Printer and Postmaster. Some Facts and Documents Relating to His Career." *Bulletin of the New York Public Library* 24 (1920), 483–99.

Payne, George H. *History of Journalism in the United States.* New York and London: D. Appleton & Co., 1920.

Phillips, J. S. R. "The Growth of Journalism." In *The Cambridge History of English Literature,* edited by A. W. Ward and A. R. Waller. 14 vols., 14:184–225. New York: G. P. Putnam's Sons, 1907–17.

Plomer, H. R., Bushnell, G. H., and Dix, E. R. McC. *A Dictionary of*

Sargent, George H. "James Rivington, Tory Printer. A Study of the *the Printers and Booksellers Who Were at Work in England, Scotland, and Ireland from 1726 to 1775.* Oxford: Oxford University Press, 1932.

Loyalist Pamphlets of the Revolution." *The American Collector* 2 (1926), 336–38.

Schlesinger, Arthur Meier. *Prelude to Independence: The Newspaper War on Britain, 1764–1776*. New York: Alfred A. Knopf, 1958.

Schuyler, Livingston R. *The Liberty of the Press in the American Colonies before the Revolutionary War, with Particular Reference to Conditions in the Royal Colony of New York*. New York: Thomas Whittaker, 1905.

Scott, Kenneth. "A British Counterfeiting Press in New York Harbor, 1776." *New-York Historical Society Quarterly* 39 (1955), 117–20.

Siebert, Fred S. "The Confiscated Revolutionary Press." *Journalism Quarterly* 13 (1936), 179–81.

Thomas, Charles M. "The Publication of Newspapers During the American Revolution." *Journalism Quarterly* 9 (1932), 358–73.

Vail, R. W. G. "The Unique *Declaration of Independence* Printed by Hugh Gaine." *New-York Historical Society Quarterly* 32 (1948), 221–24.

Walker, W. K. "Introducing H. Gaine, Provincial Grand Secretary." American Lodge of Research, Free and Accepted Masons. *Transactions* 3, no. 1 (October 31, 1938–October 30, 1939), 11–24.

Wall, Alexander J. "Early Newspapers." *New-York Historical Society Quarterly Bulletin* 15 (1931), 39–66.

———. "Samuel Loudon (1727–1813)." *New-York Historical Society Quarterly Bulletin* 6 (1922), 75–92.

Williams, J. B. "The Beginnings of English Journalism." In *The Cambridge History of English Literature*, edited by A. W. Ward and A. R. Waller. 14 vols., 2:389–415. New York: G. P. Putnam's Sons, 1907–17.

Winterich, John T. *Early American Books & Printing*. Boston and New York: Houghton Mifflin Co., 1935.

Wroth, Lawrence C. *Abel Buell of Connecticut: Silversmith, Typefounder and Engraver*. Middletown, Conn.: Wesleyan University Press, 1958.

———. *The Colonial Printer*. Portland, Me.: Southworth-Anthoensen Press, 1938.

Index

Adams, John: sees fight over bishop-ric as presaging independence, 56
Adams, Samuel: circulates "Journal of Occurences," 66; tries to keep discontent alive, 80; leads Boston Tea Party, 85; in New York, 94; mentioned, 72, 97
Addison, Joseph, 14
Administration of Justice Act, 88
Admiralty courts, 51
Advertising in *New-York Mercury:* lack of, in New Jersey, 114; mentioned, 12–13
Aix-la-Chapelle, Treaty of, 24
Albany, New York, 25, 41
Allen, Ethan: reported prisoner in England, 98; greeted by James Rivington, 135
Almanacs: printed by HG, 13, 32, 64
America: future envisioned, 48; interests said to lie in reconciliation, 101
American Booksellers Association, 137
American Chronicle: published by Samuel Farley, 30
American Literary Fair, 138
Americans: reminded of heritage of freedom, 40; unity in Stamp Act crisis, 41–42; religious observance questioned, 55; petition for repeal of Townshend Acts, 60
Anabaptists, 33

Anderson, John: publishes *Weekly Post-Boy* with Samuel Parker, 83–84; establishes *Constitutional Gazette,* 105
Anglican church: influence on Loyalists, 145
Anglicans: trustees of King's College, 15; HG prints pamphlets of, 23; bishopric proposed for colonies, 55; mentioned, 144, 145
Apprentices, 14
Apprenticeship: terms of, 2–3; conditions, 77
Ash, John, 131
Asia: fires on New York, 104

Banyar, George, 81
Barre, Isaac, 38
Bayley, Richard, 131
Belfast, Ireland, 2
Bernard, Francis: and Massachusetts General Assembly, 65; subject of forged letter, 67
Bible, Sign of the, 133
Bible and Crown, Sign of the, 23, 28, 32, 98, 106, 109, 115, 121, 146
Blair, Robert, 14
Booth, Benjamin, 85
Boston: compared to New York, 6; population, 33; opposes Stamp Act, 41, 52; celebrates Stamp Act repeal, 47; British reprisals against, 65, 88; suspected of provoking Britain, 66; HG reduces amount

of news from, 66; military occupation of, 71; leadership of Sons of
Liberty in, 72; violence in, 73; supported by HG, 88–89; mentioned,
30
Boston Common: troops quartered
on, 66
Boston Gazette: HG reprints essay
from, 51–52; HG reprints letter
from, 75
Boston massacre: HG prints radical
report, 67–68; preceded by Battle
of Golden Hill, 72
Boston merchants: agree to support
nonimportation, 57; urge New
Yorkers to end nonimportation,
62; hold to nonimportation, 63;
derided as hypocrites, 63
Boston Port Act: printed in *New-
York Mercury,* 88
Boston Tea Party, 85
Bradford, William: establishes first
press in New York, 7; begins *New-
York Gazette,* 7; apprentices of, 8;
mentioned, 79, 146
Britain: colonial policy attacked, 23;
treasury weakened by Seven Years'
War, 28; seeks American financial
support, 34; colonial policy defended in *Mercury,* 51–52; antiwar
protests in, 97; disagreement in
America on opposition to, 101;
HG imports books from, 134. *See
also* England
British: reprisals against Boston, 65;
occupation of New York, 78; warships off New York, 103; sympathizers return to New York, 135
—common law of libel: used to justify Alexander McDougall's imprisonment, 74
—occupational government: appreci-
ates Ambrose Serle's humor, 112;
forbids HG to publish news of vic-
tories, 124; appoints licenser of

press, 127; gives possible bribe to
HG, 144
—soldiers: plans for quartering in
Boston, 66; life in New York, 70;
provoke mob in New York, 71–
72; atrocities reported in *New-
York Mercury,* 97–98; land on
Long Island, 104; occupy New
York, 107; repulse French threat
to Georgia, 128; as actors, 130
British East India Company Act; pas-
sage by Parliament, 84; provisions,
84; effect on HG, 85; mentioned,
79
Broome, John, 126
Brownjohn, Dr. William, 23, 146
Brussels, Belgium, 129
Burgoyne, John, 127
Burnaby, Andrew: describes New
York, 33; on America's future, 48
Businesses: as communication centers,
14

Calvinists, 33
Campbell, Ensign: quartered in HG's
house, 119, 130
Cannon, James: writes as "Cassan-
dra," 101–2
Car, Anthony: leases *Weekly Post-
Boy* with Samuel Inslee, 79; re-
linquishes lease on *Weekly Post-
Boy,* 83; mentioned, 82
Carey, Matthew, 137
Caslon, William: type face of, 10
Catholics: not tolerated, 33
Champlain, Lake, battle of: reported
in *New-York Mercury,* 121
Chapel Street Theatre, 28
Chatham, Lord. *See* Pitt, William
Christopher, George, 13
Clinton, Fort: taken by British, 124
Clinton, George, 135
Colden, Cadwallader: attacks press in
Stamp Act crisis, 42; house ran-
sacked, 44; attacks Sons of Liberty,

Young buys HG's business, 141–
42; with William Young publishes
New York Price Current, 142;
publishes *Daily Item*, 142
Molasses Act, 34
Montcalm, Marquis de: wins Forts
Oswego and William Henry, 25
Montgomery, Fort: taken by British,
124
Moore, Henry: asks HG to print of-
ficial account of Sons of Liberty in-
cident, 69
Moore, John H., 134
Moore, Richard, 32
Moore and Neale, 114
Moravians, 33

Nancy: turns back with tea, 85
Narraway, Daniel, 77
Necessity, Fort: surrendered by
Washington, 25
Newark, New Jersey: 118; HG in,
112–13; business languishes in,
114; mentioned, 105, 106
Newark Gazette, 107
New Haven, Connecticut, 29
New Jersey: printing in, 79; printers,
107; wartime conditions in, 115–
16; mentioned, 26, 141, 144
Newport, Rhode Island: nonimporta-
tion compact in, 56
Newspaper reading: satirized in *New-
York Mercury*, 30–31
Newspapers: in Stamp Act crisis, 42;
devote more space to American af-
fairs, 79; debate independence,
100–101; Tory contents, 127
Newspaper vendors, 127
New York, province of: governors
conflict with General Assembly, 19;
"Society for the Promotion of Arts,
Agriculture and Oeconomy" formed
in, 35; HG adds coat of arms to
nameplate of *New-York Mercury*,
54; Committee of Correspondence

formed, 89; Committee of Correspondence (Albany) condemns
New-York Mercury, 92; Committee
of Observation (Suffolk County)
condemns *New-York Mercury*, 92;
Committee of Observation rebukes
Rivington, 99
—General Assembly: condemns HG,
14; votes funds for King's College,
15, 22; censures HG for printing
without permission, 18–21; conflict with governors over money,
19; Parker fears reprisals by, 21;
taxes newspapers, 24; contracts
with HG for printing of votes and
proceedings, 32; DeLancey faction,
54; awards public printer post to
HG, 54; HG as public printer for,
54–55; votes funds to garrison
British troops, 73
New York, state of: legislature
chooses HG to print money, 135;
mentioned, 104
—Committee of Safety: reprimands
Loudon, 125–26; offers HG's type
to Holt, 126; replaces Loudon as
official printer, 126; persuades Holt
to set up printing office, 126
—Provincial Congress: gives Holt
HG's type, 117; angered by Loudon, 125–26; mentioned, 105
New York Chronicle, 78, 126
New York City: Dutch influences in,
5–6; description of, 5–6, 14, 19–
20, 23, 33, 118–19; population, 6;
printers, 7; politics, 14; education
in, 15; press unrestricted in 18th-
century, 19; threatened by French,
25; on eve of prosperity, 28; theater, 28, 130, 138–39; landmarks,
33; in Sugar Act crisis, 34–36;
celebrates Stamp Act repeal, 47;
amusements, 50; Fort George as
British garrison, 70; common council disapproves erection of liberty